"A profoundly personal, realistically practical statement about spirituality as part of the human condition."

Dr. Reginald Stackhouse,
Principal Emeritus and Research Professor
Wycliffe College, University of Toronto

"Jack writes an inspiring and helpful book on spiritual development. The aim of this book is to help the reader explore practical ideas for path-breaking spiritual solutions. This book is filled with wonderful revelations that form the cornerstone of timeless truths."

Dr. Tracy Austin, Ph.D
Psychotherapist, Toronto

"Jack McQuaig, clearly inspired by a higher source, is a successful businessman who incorporates spiritual principles into all aspects of his life. I see the proof of his path in that he is able to balance the spiritual and the material, fully integrated, established and respected in society. Too often we are taking the spiritual advice of those who cannot cope with the world today. Jack McQuaig offers simple, practical advice to help anyone along the path of love, the unfolding of the symbolic petals of the soul within this temple we call our bodies."

Dr. Heather A. Tomlin, M.D., C.C.F.P.

of your excellent presentation at the Forum
Sincerely Jack

"In this production the author of many 'How to' books looks in an entirely different direction. Major companies in many countries have implemented the advice provided by his writings on management executive thinking, profiting in business and human relations. Now, McQuaig turns to the intensely personal aspects of the individual, based on his own ponderings about life, its meaning, and its possibilities for spiritual quality. He writes as one outside denominationalism or as an adherent of any of the world's major religions. He is a seeker after truth and has found some answers. His purpose is to share what he has discovered for the benefit of others."

General Arnold Brown, OC
Retired International Leader,
The Salvation Army.

"Jack McQuaig has spent his career helping to bring out the best in people. He now brings a lifetime of experience and observation to this practical guide to the spiritual path. Jack has an intensely personal commitment to this subject and is an inspiring example of wholism and health: mind, body and spirit."

Dr. Ruth Anne Baron, N.D.
North Toronto Naturopathic Clinic

"Written out of the accumulated wisdom, experience and practice of his many years, Jack McQuaig provides a perceptive and practical guide for all who wish to move further along the road of spiritual fitness"

The Rev. William J. Middleton, M.A.,B.D.
Minister, Armour Heights Presbyterian Church

ON THE PATH TO SPIRITUAL FITNESS

Also by Jack H.McQuaig

How to Pick Men
Frederick Fell Inc.

How to Motivate Men
Frederick Fell Inc.

How to Interview and Hire Productive People
(with Peter L. and Donald H. McQuaig)
Frederick Fell Inc.

Challenge Yourself and Live
General Publishing

Your Business, Your Son and You
B. Klein Publications

The Pregnant Male
Hunter Carlyle Publishing

Synergy and the Power of Personal Proficiency
Hunter Carlyle Publishing

Like Yourself and Live
Hunter Carlyle Publishing

Keep Feeling Good with Mental Fitness
Hunter Carlyle Publishing

ON THE PATH TO SPIRITUAL FITNESS

Jack H. McQuaig

HUNTER CARLYLE PUBLISHING

The author or endorsers or the publisher, or anyone whose name appears in this book, will not be liable to anyone in regard to any loss or damage said to be caused directly or indirectly by the information in this book.

Jack McQuaig is not a Minister, Priest, Rabbi or a Sunday School Teacher. Before you make any changes in your attitudes or life style consult with your spiritual counselor. The advice, information and guidelines presented in this book are not intended to replace professional medical care. Before you make any changes in your health regime, check with your doctor.

Canadian Cataloguing in Publication Data

McQuaig, Jack H.
On the path to spiritual fitness

ISBN 0-9691113-6-3

1. Spirituality. 2. Spiritual life. I. Title

BV4501.2.M343 2000 248 C00-931852-6

Hunter Carlyle Publishing
One Queen Street East,
Toronto, ON M5C 2W5

Typesetting and Design: Robin Brass Studio

Printed and bound in Canada by AGMV-Marquis,
Cap-Saint-Ignace, Quebec.

In memory of my mother

Zoe

A great Lady

FOREWORD

The last decade before the third millenium has been characterized by a resurgence of interest in spirituality. This quest has taken numerous forms, including the search for human rootedness in nature and the affirmation of meaning and integrity in business and social behavior. It is in this latter category that this book by Jack McQuaig finds its place.

McQuaig, a successful business executive, documents the sources of his own spiritual quest in the everyday corporate world of making decisions, finding inner solace, relating to people and communing with the Higher Being. He has read scores of books, listened to countless talks and tapes, and has come up with principles to affirm the things worth knowing in a world of compromise and easy solutions. He hopes you will join him in this pilgrimage for things spiritual and eternal

I would be surprised if, after reading the book and savoring the quest, you haven't found a score of golden nuggets for your own soul and spirit.

EUGENE BANNERMAN
Professor of Psychology
Ryerson Polytechnic University
Toronto, Ontario

CONTENTS

ACKNOWLEDGEMENTS

I want to thank the many acquaintances and friends who have shared with me their ideas on religion and spirituality.

In particular, I would like to mention the following who have gone beyond the call of duty in helping me put this book together. Ren Donaldson, Dr. Tracy Austin, Lee Sargeant, Rowena Van Seters, Tammy Gelfand, Dr. Irving Walkoff, Log McQuaig, Linda McQuaig, Wendy Fallis, Don McQuaig, Peter McQuaig, Dr. Heather Tomlin, Dr. Ruth Baron, Dr. Eugene Bannerman, Sharon Smith and General Arnold Brown.

Marni Jones, my assistant at the office, has done a spectacular job in getting my thoughts into print and keeping me thinking in a practical way.

ON THE PATH TO SPIRITUAL FITNESS

INTRODUCTION

Why am I writing this book? I am writing it to provide a spiritual concept that I hope will appeal to every one. I am hoping my philosophy will be helpful to those of any religion or creed who want to move further along the path to spiritual fitness. I am also hoping to be of help to those who aren't even on the path.

What is spiritual fitness? It is the feeling that God is within you at all times. It's the acceptance of the world as God is running it. It's surrendering your life and all your problems to God and practicing his philosophy of loving others, helping them in their day to day life and contributing something to the world. It's having peace of mind and happiness.

I must warn all of my readers that I am not trained in any religious doctrine. I am not a Priest, Rabbi, Monk or Minister. I don't have a Ph.D. in religious theory nor do I have any experience as a lay minister or even as a Sunday School teacher. I am not a prophet, priest or guru, nor do I have any more influence or connection with God than anyone else. I was exposed to Christian teaching as a boy in the Presbyterian Church. My mother, who was a dedicated Christian, made sure that I went to church and Sunday School every

Sunday until I was 14 or 15. Then I abandoned church except when, in later years, I took my children to Sunday school. Since then my life has been lived as an agnostic until five years ago when I began work on this book and developed a faith in God.

My experience has been mainly in the world of business and psychology. I have attempted during my working career to bring the science of psychology into the business world to assist business managers to develop better methods of hiring, motivating and developing people. I had reasonable success in the business world and developed three small businesses in the areas of selecting, motivating and counseling personnel.

However, since my semi-retirement I have been able to concentrate more on the philosophies and theories that interest me most and I find myself each day turning more and more to the study of spirituality to find the keys to happiness and peace of mind. As I get older, I see clearly that making money, achieving power and developing skills do not give me the answer to happiness and peace of mind.

I am a relative newcomer on the path to spiritual fitness. I am a believer in a Supreme Being, who is running the universe. I will refer to this Supreme Being as God or the Spiritual Force but many of you may refer to her or him with other names. I believe that God is a form of Divine Person superior in every way to human beings. God could be male or female but to simplify the references to God, I will refer to him as male. In referring to the people in this book, I will use female in one chapter and male in the next.

I have started on the path to spiritual fitness but I am not there yet. The progress I have made however convinces me that there is a God or Spiritual Force who loves us and wants us to be happy. So I hope we can proceed together and learn together. I want to write something that will be helpful to all my readers, spiritual, or nonspiritual because we are all capable of moving towards spiritual fitness.

My purpose in writing this book is to try to simplify spirituality. I have discovered a method of entering the spiritual world, which will be easy to understand and free of ritual, fear, theory and tradition. It is a system which all men and women can understand so they can get the feeling of spirituality in their lives and achieve a philosophy of living which will enable them to love others, help others, contribute something to the world and gain peace of mind and happiness.

My basic concept is that each person is a worldly self, a spiritual self or a worldly spiritual self. The worldly self believes that she is her body, mind and personality. She is concerned with the outer world and with achieving, gaining power, developing skills, accumulating money and competing with others in all areas of life. This doesn't mean that the worldly self is bad. Many people who are successful in worldly activities lead ethical, honest lives. Often they contribute to charities with effort and money and help the underprivileged.

However, the worldly self doesn't believe in the spiritual. She is unable to accept anything that does not conform to worldly logic and reality.

The spiritual person on the other hand has faith and belief in a God that is beyond the grasp of the worldly self. The spiritual self is concerned with giving, helping others, contributing to the world and loving all people and all living things. The spiritual person does not concentrate on the outcome of money accumulation, attainment of power and skill development. She is concerned more with integrity, serenity and quality and concentrates on the present and the process of what she is doing rather than on the outcome. However, by being concerned with the process, the spiritual self often achieves great success in the outer world.

The spiritual person concentrates on her inner world and being in touch with her soul in her day to day performance. Although the spiritual person is living in the world, she is not of the world. Her mind and heart are always concentrating on the spiritual and the great Universal Power. She believes in a world beyond the five senses. Through her belief in God she can do things that seem impractical and unrealistic to the worldly person. She has faith.

For example, as a spiritually fit person she feels that God is constantly guiding her and empowering her. When she is frustrated in achieving something she surrenders to God and he takes over the problem. She believes that God is operating the world and she accepts the world as it is and adjusts to it without stress. She is relatively worry free because she believes that God will look after her.

Some people are living the life of the worldly self; others are living the life of the spiritual. There is another type of person, whom I call the worldly spiritual. She is living at times the spiritual life and at other times the worldly life. She is not completely spiritual or completely worldly.

Each person in addition to being worldly, spiritual, or worldly-spiritual, has an ego. The ego is sort of an imaginary being. It is who the person is trying to be. It is her attempt to put her best foot forward by trying to be right and successful and important. The ego is proud and will fight to be right. The ego isn't concerned with the welfare of other people. It doesn't care about others losing or being unhappy, as long as it wins. The ego operates in a win lose world. The ego tends to believe in the theory that winning is everything and it will do just about anything to win, even if it means humiliating others. Unfortunately, most of the things we are taught in the educational, family and social worlds are attempts to build the ego and make the individual successful at all costs in the outer world.

Unfortunately, the ego tends to be negative in its attitudes and is always trying to kill spiritual goals with negative thoughts. One of the big problems in getting to spiritual fitness is to get control of the ego. You don't want to destroy your ego, but rather get it under control, so it will stop sabotaging your advancement to spiritual fitness. The ego hates spirituality and will do anything to keep you from it, because once you accept the spiritual self and enjoy happiness and peace of mind, you will eliminate the ego's need to be important and to win at all costs.

In order to retain control, your ego will constantly ridicule the benefits of the Higher Self. It will also fill your mind with distressing thoughts and images of what life can do to you unless you struggle for more money, more power, more skill and more winning over others. I don't want to indicate that the ego is all bad. Maybe your very existence depends on it. The ego will give you confidence and help you to achieve and to win but it puts too much weight on self aggrandizement.

It usually takes a long time to overcome some of the selfish drives of the ego and come into the joy of living with the spiritual self. The ego's attitude is "What's in it for me?" The attitude of the spiritual person is "How may I serve?" This book is designed to help you to get control of the ego and embrace the spiritual as soon as possible.

Physical health and mental health are both very important for spiritual fitness. A healthy body and mind will help you to become what you want to become. You feel better, you think better and you can become a stronger person with a sound mind and body. The spiritual person believes that her mind and body were given to her as gifts from God and it is her duty to maintain them in as close to perfect form as possible.

There are many Spiritual leaders and many religions that will lead you to God. Wherever your faith lies, keep with it. God has many saints bringing people to him via different religions. These are all paths to God and most of them will lead you to God. Because of the great variety in men and women, many different types of religion are needed to attract people to God. Whatever track you are on, stay with it if it is bringing you to God. I have no desire to change your belief. However if you don't believe in any God or follow any Spiritual leader or religion and want to have faith in something maybe this book will help you.

My God is filled with love and understanding. My God is a spiritual power within you who doesn't criticize or punish. My God wants you to do what you want and to be happy. If you do what you think is wrong, you will punish yourself. You create your own heaven and hell in your mind.

What my God expects of you is that you love yourself and everyone unconditionally and that you dedicate your life to the service of others and to improving the world. If you do these three things you can't be doing anything wrong. You will be leading an ideal life without being threatened with punishment and you should be happy and have peace of mind.

In my form of spirituality the Bible is considered one of the greatest books that was ever written. It has many ideas, which we can use. It has many interesting parables and stories. My religion will use parts of the Bible but it will also use modern books like. *A Return to Love*, by Marianne Williamson, *Real Magic*, by Wayne Dyer, *Ageless Body, Timeless Mind*,by Deepak Choppra, *The Seat of the Soul*, by Gary Zukov, *End the Struggle and Dance with Life*, by Susan Jeffers, *Timeless Healing*, by Herbert Benson, *The Road Less Traveled and Beyond*, by M. Scott Peck, *The Power Within You*, by Louise L. Hay, *Love is the Answer*, by Gerald G. Jampolsky and Diane V. Cirincione, *Pray as You Go*, by Robert Meneilly, and *Spiritual Growth*,by Sanaya Roman.

My spirituality is centered in God and is easy to understand. It will concentrate on the present and the future, rather than the past. My spirituality should make people who embrace it, very happy. They will feel that God loves them, forgives them and cares for them. There are no commandments to follow, and no punishment to bear.

If you get on the path to spiritual fitness you will feel that God is always within you, loving you, caring for you and guiding you. You will surrender to God and let him run the world. You will feel that God is empowering you. You will love yourself and others, help others and realize that we are all connected spiritually. Accepting others as they are without criticism and blame and forgiving them is the essence of the spiritual way.

These are very idealistic requirements and for this reason it is very difficult to get on the path to spiritual fitness and to stay on the path and keep progressing. It requires constant commitment to keep your thinking and attitudes on track. To become spiritually fit you need to think of God constantly, spending as much time as possible each day praying, meditating, reading spiritual books, writing about the spiritual and listening to spiritual tapes or sermons. However, the rewards are great and those who move to the Higher Self and get their egos under control are happy and have peace of mind. They get along well with others, make good friends and build solid relationships. It is worth trying to behave like the Higher Self and I hope my formula will help those who wish to achieve this goal.

In this book I am giving you one way to achieve spiritual fitness or the Higher Self status and I am suggesting the words to use and the pictures to visualize in order to attain this goal. This formula has worked for me and helped me to get on the path to spiritual fitness. For you I hope it will be a guide. I don't expect you to follow it exactly but I hope you may borrow from it to help you formulate your own program and gain the advantages of being spiritually fit. Very few people achieve this outcome but the constant struggle for it is important. My goal is to have you dream the possible dream and achieve spiritual fitness. This state I call Godliness.

If you do achieve spiritual fitness, don't expect the world to be a different place. You will still have all the problems of living but spiritual fitness will give you the attitudes to enable you to go through life with less distress and tension than before you became spiritually fit.

WHY I BELIEVE IN GOD, A SPIRITUAL FORCE

The most powerful conviction that there is a God, has come to me through prayer. I believe in prayer. I find it therapeutic. Whenever I pray, I feel that I am talking to God. But what really convinced me of the validity of prayer was when I read Larry Dossey's book *Healing Words* in which he describes some of the research that has been done on prayer. In this book Dr. Dossey gives unquestionable evidence that prayer works. In many cases under laboratory conditions it has been proven that prayer does have the power to influence situations and make real changes; sometimes dramatic changes.

In one piece of research, Cardiologist Ralph Byrd selected by computer 192 patients admitted to a San Francisco Hospital. These patients were then prayed for by regular homecare meetings taking place throughout the U.S.A. They didn't know they were being prayed for. He selected another group of 201 patients who were not being prayed for.

The results of this study were amazing. The patients in the group that were being prayed for were five times less likely to require antibiotics and three times less likely to develop complications. These results were confirmed by Dr. William Nolan, a physician who attempts to expose false claims of faithhealers and miracle workers in medicine. He said the study stood up to standard methods of scientific investigation. This was one of hundreds of cases where prayers were proven to work as described in Dr. Dossey's book.

The fact that scientific experiments prove that prayer works convinces me definitely that there is a God or a Spiritual Force. Who else could make prayer work except God?

We also have scientific evidence for the validity of meditation. Experience with meditation convinces me that there is a God. During meditation, I feel the presence of God and I have received some good answers to some of my questions put to God during these sessions. Meditation brings me a feeling that is far above the normal day to day reaction that I get from the five senses.

Meditation is the situation in which you listen to God. Instead of thanking God and asking for his help as you do in prayer, you sit quietly, and concentrate on silence so God can communicate with you. You will get the feeling of God's presence, if you do it right.

In his book *Creative Meditation*, Richard Peterson describes the work of Michael Murphy and Steven Donovan in their book, *The Physical and Physiological effects of Meditation a Review and Comprehensive Bibliography 1931-1988*, in which the authors describe the results of hundreds of validated research projects showing the benefits of meditation.

Daniel Goldman, a psychologist, in his book, The *Meditation Mind: The Varieties of Meditation Experience*, summarizes some of the physical and physiological effects of meditation. (1). It causes a drop in blood pressure (2). It relieves suffering from angina and arrhythmia and lowers blood cholesterol levels (3) It may increase the immune functions of the body, increasing defense against colds, flu, pneumonia and other infectious diseases.

There are other meditative studies according to Richard Peterson which indicate that it has many psychological benefits, such as (1) Decrease in neurotic tendencies, (2) Improvement in study efficiency and exam performance, (3) Improvement in creativity in the visual arts, (4) Decrease in drug and alcohol abuse.

If any of these benefits of meditation are true something must be causing them. Who else but God could cause such profound effects on the human body from a simple technique like meditation? This convinces me that there is a great spiritual power who is operating the universe. Call him or her God, Allah, the Spiritual Force or any other name.

Intuition has also strengthened my belief in God. Several times my intuition has given me a strong urge to take some action. At one time I heard a homeopathic doctor give a lecture on health. Although the fees seemed high and the inconvenience great, my intuition kept urging me to go and consult with this doctor which I did. The result was the discovery for me of a new way of health. My advice to you is to pay attention to your intuition. It is one of God's methods of communicating with you. Yes, I believe there is a God.

All the great spiritual masters admit that love is at the heart of their religion or philosophy. They all believe that God is a God of love and that most of our problems could be solved if we would turn to love. This has been proven to be true in my life. In several situations in which I was having conflicts with others, I was able to resolve these problems and have good relationships by sending love to these people. This convinces me that God is with me in these situations. Otherwise, how could this magic happen?

My approach in using love to heal a relationship has been to visualize myself getting along well with the person with whom I am in conflict. I see clearly in my mind that we are relating well before I come in contact with the person. When we meet, I concentrate on his strengths and talk to him about those things. I accept his behavior, whatever it is without any judgment or criticism. I try to work in some comment like "I like your style" or "I like the way you do things" or any comment that will show him that I like him. If he talks, I listen very carefully and if I get an opportunity I ask his opinion or his advice. During our meeting I try to smile and thank him for anything he has done for me. As a result of this behavior our conflict is usually cleared up very quickly.

I believe the recommendations of all the great religious leaders are right. God is a God of love and forgiveness. If you want to solve any people problems, loving and forgiving are the best ways to do it. This amazing feeling of love must come from God. Who else could instigate such a wonderful outcome?

The other big concept of all religions is that service is important. Most religions suggest that your life should have a purpose. The purpose is to give service to others and put service above self. Once you practice this in your day to day life you will start to feel better.

To test this proposition I set up a practical situation where

I could practice giving to others and see if it made any change in my life. Up until this time I would often pass beggars on the street, give them nothing and think to myself , "Why doesn't he go to the Red Cross or the City Food Bank?" or "why doesn't he get a job?"

My new approach is to take plenty of change in my pocket each morning and whenever I encounter a beggar, I give him a coin, sometimes I even walk half a block out of my way to give to a beggar if I see him in the distance. The result is a great feeling of satisfaction. I feel good about myself and it is a worthwhile exercise. Isn't God behind this glowing feeling I get. Who else could make such a thing happen.

Alcoholics Anonymous was founded in the early forties by Bill Wilson and Dr. Robert Smith. The philosophy of Alcoholics Anonymous was to get alcoholics talking to one another, sharing their experiences and trying to help one another give up drinking. At first the idea didn't work. Sometimes alcoholics could give up drinking but they would start up again at a later date. In the beginning members of AA were required to reform themselves and become ideal people. This didn't work. Only when they accepted themselves with their weaknesses and limitations and believed that God would help them were they able to get control.

Doesn't this experience that alcoholics could only control their drinking by surrendering to God, prove that God exists?

When I look up at the sky at night and see the moon and the stars and when I notice the beautiful sunshine in the daytime, I say to myself "someone is operating this." Also, when I look at the great natural beauties of the world, it makes me think some super power is behind it all. The trees, the flowers, the plants, the rocks, the mountains, the streams, the lakes and the rivers have a God like quality and make me realize there is some super intelligence operating it all. The odds against this all happening by chance or by accident are overwhelming.

When I look back over my life, I find many things that I was forced to do, which I didn't want to do at the time, which eventually turned out to be a great help to me in moving along the road I wanted to travel. For example, a girl I loved once deserted me which caused me great distress. Eventually, I met another girl who was much better for me. Once I failed to get a promotion, which I wanted badly however this gave me the idea of starting my own business, which made a wonderful career for me.

I have counted 32 situations like this in my life. These were situations, which forced me to do something different than I wanted to do, but something, which was better for me in my attempt to achieve my goals. I feel that these frustrations which turned out to be for the best were no accident. God is operating the world his way and it took me sometime to stop resisting the way he is doing it.

Dr. Wayne Dyer in his writings and tapes urges his readers and listeners to surrender and let God run the world. He claims that he does this and constantly feels a Divine Presence in his life. This motivated me to stop trying to run the world. When I did this I felt secure in my behavior and convinced that there is someone operating this intelligent system and it is easier for me to surrender to it than to try to do it my way. This again convinced me that there is a God.

As I began to believe I might be guided by a Spiritual Force I began to notice things happening in my life, which were helping me to achieve my goals. For example, I was looking for information on "affirmations" for this book. These are statements which can influence your subconscious mind, if you repeat them often enough and with enough enthusiasm. In spite of my searching, I was unable to find information on this topic.

One day when I was on the subway reading a book entitled *Conversations with God*, a woman sitting next to me leaned over and asked me where I got the book. I handed it to her and told her where I bought it. She studied the cover and wrote down the name of the author and publisher. Then she asked me if I had read another book and she pulled out of her purse, a book by Douglas Block entitled *Words That Heal*. This was a book about affirmations.

What a coincidence, or was I being guided? There were at least 10 cars on the subway train and 100 seats in the car I entered. Besides this particular train, there were similar trains stopping every five minutes. Just by chance I was reading *Conversations with God* and just by chance, this woman sitting next to me had the book on affirmations in her purse. The odds on all these coincidences coming together are astronomical. This makes me wonder if I am being guided. I have had many coincidences like this. If I am being guided, only God could do it.

As I go through life I feel a presence in my body. I feel as if there is an infinite power running through me, which gives me strength at times. I notice this presence also when I have a tough problem that is worrying me. I do what I can to solve it and then I surrender it to God. This works for me and I am convinced there is a God who is taking these problems off my shoulders.

Unfortunately, I do not have this Divine Presence all the time and I am constantly striving to get it. I have only felt it on some occasions. However, I do know people who feel this Divine Presence in their lives all the time. They describe it as constant joy and happiness because God is with them, helping, guiding and empowering them. Since there is such a thing as a Divine Presence in the lives of some, it could only be inspired by God.

At one time I was very worried about some surgery that my doctor had recommended. Six months before the surgery I was feeling considerable distress just thinking about it. Suddenly, one day I said to myself "Surrender, stop worrying, let God take charge and he will bring you through this ordeal." By persisting in this thinking, I was able to stop worrying. It was a great relief to feel that God was with me loving me and caring for me. By doing this I forgot about my operation until the day I appeared at the hospital. There must be a God or I would not have been able to avoid this distress.

I believe many of the good feelings we have in life are God's way of motivating us to do what is good for us. For example, whenever we do any assignment well, whether it be at work, sports or in social situations, we get a favorable type of stress, known as eustress. My thinking is that God arranges these good feelings for work well done so we will work hard on any assignment to complete it successfully, so we will be productive in our lives and able to survive.

You will notice that we always get good feelings when we eat or drink. God gives us these feelings to encourage us to eat and drink to help us survive. We will also get feelings of satisfaction when we learn something or create something new in writing, dancing, singing, painting or playing a musical instrument. This is designed by God to encourage us to think and to pursue different activities, so we will learn and become more capable of earning a living and enjoying life.

A great feeling comes from touching another person or hugging him or her. The ultimate good feeling, of course, is from sexual intercourse. God has provided this ecstatic pleasure in order to keep us procreating so the human race will survive. When we see all the things that give us satisfaction and pleasure, which motivate us to do things which are good for us, it is obvious that somebody has designed this system. Who else could do it but God?

Dr. Raymond Moody, MD, a psychiatrist who has written several books on Near Death Experiences, claims that of about 2500 people whom he has interviewed who have had these experiences, all reported a very ecstatic joyful feeling while they were dead and they didn't want to come back to earth. Carl Jung, the great psychologist who had a near death experience, was asked if he believed in God. "No" he said, " I don't believe there is a God, I know there is a God."

A near death experience or N.D.E. is where a person is pronounced dead by medical doctors but who isn't really dead. His spirit or soul has merely left his body temporarily and he has the experience of dying. He usually has a vision of another world, where he sees bright lights and his life history runs through his mind and he often meets angels. The main feature of the near death experience is that one feels ecstatic joy and happiness, and usually when he is pulled back to earth to re-enter his body and proceed with his life, he doesn't want to come back. He is happier dead than alive. What this indicates to those who observe the phenomena is that there is a life after death and the soul never dies.

In his book, *Life After Life*, Dr. Moody describes many near death experiences. All this information on N.D.E.s convinces me that there is a Supernatural Power or God beyond the earth waiting to receive us when we shed our physical bodies and return to our spiritual habitat beyond the earth. Yes I am convinced there is a God.

One of the most interesting N.D.E., experiences is told by Denion Brinkley in his book *Saved By The Light*. Brinkley had two experiences with N.D.E.'s and at one stage in his life when he came back from a N.D.E. he had the capacity to read minds. His total experience with N.D.E. was favorable and relieved his fear of death and convinced him that there is life after death.

In his book, *Timeless Healing*, Dr. Herbert Benson M.D., tells of hundreds of validated studies which proved that people who believed in a spiritual power had much better health than those who were non-believers. Surely this indicates that there is a God who is supporting those who believe.

Most of the great Spiritual leaders like Jesus, Joan of Arc, Confucius, Mother Teresa, and Muhammad all believed in a God or Allah. If these experts in spirituality believed shouldn't you and I be believers? Even great philosophers who were scientifically inclined, like Plato, Aristotle, and Thomas Aquinas, believed in God.

Christian Science is a religion which has a reputation for curing people of incurable diseases if they can believe in God and surrender to him all concern about their health. The book *Healing Spiritually* published by the Christian Science Publishing Co. is filled with case histories of people suffering great physical distress from diseases and accidents who have cured themselves of their disabilities by praying and trusting God to cure them. Surely this is convincing evidence that there is a God.

Isn't there something magic in a relationship, where two people get together and relate positively to one another. You say "the chemistry is right" or "they are on the same wave length." It is more than two people coming together. There is a Supernatural Power involved. If they have a sexual relationship, they may produce a child. Isn't this great magic? Only God could enable two people to unite, to produce a third person.

There is also a supernatural feeling in church or in spiritual meetings. There is something magic about a group of people gathering to talk about spirituality. God is involved. The Bible is a most God like book because it is entirely about God's relationship with people. Doesn't the fact that such a brilliant book exists indicate that God must exist to have inspired it. There are so many inspiring passages which lift you up and express ideas that you feel are right on target with your own experience. I believe that God inspired the Bible.

Maybe the best evidence that there is a God is the fact that you exist. Here you are asking if there is a God. Who created you? It must have been God. You couldn't be here asking questions about God if he hadn't created you.

Many scientists over the years have been convinced that there is no God. In recent years, however, with research into atomic energy and quantum physics, most scientists now believe there is a God. Only a person with God like powers could be operating the universe successfully.

Frank J. Tiples, in his book, *Physics of Immortality*, devised a mathematical model of the end of the universe which proved that there is a God. Tiples used the most advanced methods of modern physics. He proved that God exists in the same way that scientists prove other things by research.

I have given you some evidence to prove there is a God. There is more. Every day I am convinced by some situation or action that God is in charge and running the world in his own way.

The visible marks of extraordinary wisdom and power appear so plainly in all the works of the creation that a rational creature who will but seriously reflect on them, cannot miss the discovery of a deity.

John Locke (1632-1704)

The visible order of the Universe proclaims a supreme intelligence.

J.J. Rousseau (1712-1778)

All things speak of God.

Edward Young (1683-1765)

It is impossible to account for the creation of the Universe without the agency of a supreme being.

George Washington (1732-1799)

I find in the Universe so many forms of order, organization, system, law and adjustment of means to ends, that I believe in a cosmic intelligence and I conceive God is the life, mind, order and law of the world.

Will Durant

THE SPIRITUAL PERSON

When we talk about the spiritual are we talking about religion? Not necessarily. The spiritual is beyond religion. Religions are dogmas. They provide different beliefs of the spiritual. Each religion feels that it has a monopoly on the spiritual, which makes it the fast track to salvation. The spiritual, on the other hand, belongs to all religions and to all people and does not have any dogmas or even an "800" number. Religions are paths to the spiritual but no religion has a monopoly on the spiritual. You can be a spiritual person and practice spiritual ways without believing in any particular religion. The spiritual is a way of life. Religion is a particular way of life, using the spiritual as its foundation. The spiritual is for everybody regardless of religion or creed.

Here are some attitudes and beliefs of the spiritual person.

1. *She is connected to the Power of the Universe*

The person who leads a spiritual life feels the constant connection with Universal Power by always feeling the spiritual power from the universe running through her body. This is known as the Divine Presence. Whenever she is discouraged depressed or feeling rejected she repeats her conditioning statement which may be something like this." ***Thank you God for being within me, and bringing the power of the Universe flowing through me. Thank you God. I love you God."*** She also uses this affirmation or some variation of it when she is in a good state of mind. She uses it constantly because she wants to get into the habit of always feeling that God is within her ready to help her with any problem.

With the constant feeling of this supernatural power flowing through her, she faces life with confidence and determination. Whenever her mind strays into negative thoughts she brings it back to positive thinking by repeating the affirmation.

To help her with this method of knowing that God is always with her, she pretends that there is a muscle pulling her mind from negative thoughts to the positive thought of being connected to Universal Power. The more she uses this muscle the more strength it will gain to pull her back to her connection with God. Eventually this imaginary muscle will get so strong that it will automatically switch from negative thoughts to the thought of Universal Power flowing through her.

As she goes through life she feels that she is in the world but not of the world. This means that in everything she does in her day to day activity, she approaches it from the point of view of a spiritual person attached to the great Universal Power. This enables her to experience life more objectively and she becomes somewhat detached and less emotional about her life experiences. This doesn't mean she has less interest in the things she is doing but she approaches everything in a more relaxed manner and with less intensity.

2. *She is motivated by her inner life*

She believes that she can control her life to a large degree by controlling her thoughts visualizations and intentions.. She goes inward and concentrates on visualizing and self-talk, thinking and talking to herself about life the way she intends it to be. She realizes that every action in life is preceded by a thought and to think and plan in her mind what she wants to do, is the first step in making it come true. The next step is to activate her intention to do it. She believes her intention reinforced by the pictures in her mind, will make it happen. Her intention to make things happen energizes the pictures in her mind and brings them into reality.

The spiritual person knows that what she focuses on in her mind expands. If she starts having negative thoughts about the future that will expand. For example, if she worries about getting sick and going to the hospital and keeps visualizing this happening, she will probably get sick and go to the hospital. So she concentrates on being healthy and well and visualizing herself living to 105 years old and passing away in her sleep.

She believes that happiness and peace of mind depend more on her intentions and attitudes than on her external environment. If she is thinking the right thoughts backed up with positive attitudes, positive visualizing and positive intentions, she will feel good even in a bad environment, but if she has negative attitudes and envisions bad things in her internal world, she will feel badly even in a favorable environment. So she keeps working on her internal attitudes, visions and intentions, so bad environments cause her less stress.

She believes that her life is programed by the pictures in her mind and by her intentions. If her life doesn't turn out the way she visualizes it, she realizes that this is God's will and she adjusts silently to it.

3. *She surrenders*

The spiritual person tries her best in every situation in which she is involved. However, when she can't solve a problem she surrenders it to God. She believes that God is ready to help her in any situation provided she has tried her best and then surrenders to him. It is a great strength to the spiritual person to know that she has constant help available in any situation. It helps her to avoid worrying.

4. *She adjusts to the World as it is*

The spiritual person believes God is operating the world his way. She tries to adjust to things as they are. She tries to change the things she can and leaves the rest to God. Some spiritual masters say that spiritual fitness is the acceptance of things as they are. This may be an oversimplification but adjusting to the world as God is operating it, is certainly a step forward on the path to spiritual fitness.

The spiritual person doesn't like some of what she sees in the world. The poverty, brutality, war, killing, rape, divorce and separation are all things she will try to eliminate. However her attitude is positive. She understands that God knows things that she doesn't know and there is a reason for everything.

5. *She believes her life has a purpose*

She believes that she was put on this earth for some specific reason. The reason is to love others and to serve them and to contribute to the improvement of the world. She doesn't expect to get anything out of this world. She can't take anything with her. She concentrates on what she can contribute. What can she give? When giving is her sole purpose, her life takes on a new direction. She stops striving for more and avoids trying to out do others. She has a philosophy of life which can be summed up in three words "***service above self.***" This attitude gives her a big purpose in life and helps keep her morale high and her motivation strong.

With this attitude towards life the spiritual person often achieves great things or attracts great wealth. Often she gets more material things than the non-spiritual person although she is not pushing in this direction. She puts service to her fellow men and women and her community, ahead of herself and in doing this she often proves that "***she profits most who serves the best.***" She works to a standard of excellence and is more concerned with doing things well than with making money or achieving status. Integrity and quality are important to her and she refuses to compromise her ethics in order to achieve any goal. She is more concerned with the quality of life she leads than with what goal she achieves.

6. *She has high self esteem*

She knows that loving herself has nothing to do with conceit, assertiveness, aggressiveness, or any tendencies to self aggrandizement or showing off. These traits are all symptoms of not liking herself. She knows that self-esteem is not self-confidence nor is it attained by achievement, money, fame or great skill. She knows that self-esteem is the feeling that she is a worth while person just because she is herself. She believes that she was created by the great Spiritual Force and has within her this unlimited greatness. This knowledge makes her feel good about herself and she loves herself.

7. *She believes she is being guided*

In reviewing her life she has found many situations where she has been frustrated in her desire to do something and was forced to do it another way which eventually turned out to be better for her. These situations have convinced her that God is always with her and guiding her in her best interests. For example, at one stage in her life she had a job, which she loved. Unfortunately she was released from this job. At the time it seemed like a tragedy, but it turned out to be good for her because it caused her to continue her education at University and to become a professional social worker. This gave her a better career in the long run.

8. *She concentrates on the present*

The spiritual person tries to concentrate on the present. Prayer is her greatest help in doing this. She knows that God is not a judging, punishing, individual but the epitome of love and understanding. She knows she can surrender to him her regrets about the past and worries about the future, while she concentrates on enjoying the present.

She knows that when she is constantly concentrating on the present she is not alone. God is guiding her and empowering her to have peace of mind and happiness.

At one time a famous guru claimed that he was always happy and joyful. When asked how he was able to attain this state he claimed that he never thought about the past or the future but always concentrated on the present.

One of the most important aspects of the spiritual life is trust in ourselves and trust in God. By concentrating on the present and listening to our inner feelings with God always with us we develop the habit of trusting. We may find things changing as we live in the present. We may stop worrying about the past and the future. We may get the feeling that everything is going to work out the way we want it. We know that God is guiding us and we can surrender and let him deal with those problems we cannot solve.

9. *She is a giving person*

All the great religious and spiritual concepts have three important beliefs in common. They all believe that loving others, giving and helping others and contributing to the community are the basic drives of spirituality. The spiritual person believes in giving and helping. She is always alert to situations in which she can contribute to the welfare of others and to the environment in which she lives.

She keeps money in circulation. She gives away anything she is not using. Each time she visits a friend or relative she takes a gift of some kind. She gives for her own sake as much as for the sake of others. For example, if she is trying to decide how much to give for a tip or to a charity, she always gives the larger amount. Giving makes her feel good about herself. She believes in sharing the wealth.

10. *She follows her intuition*

The spiritual person believes in intuition. She believes that her mind is connected with the Spiritual Force. At times she has strong feelings or hunches about something and she has learned to pay attention to these feelings. Often she will get a feeling that she should take certain action. She usually finds that unless she follows these strong feelings she will not achieve what she wants. At a later date she usually finds that her hunches were right. She doesn't always follow her intuitive hunches but she always examines them carefully.

For example, at one time when her mother was sick in the hospital she visited her occasionally. One night she had a strong feeling that she should go and see her mother immediately. This intuitive feeling was so great that she drove a long distance to visit her mother, whom she found in a very distressed condition.

11. *She is a forgiving person*

She knows that forgiveness is the way to improve relations with others. When you forgive someone your attitude towards them changes from one of wanting to retaliate to one of love and understanding. The forgiving person knows that everyone is doing the best they can with their limited wisdom and blaming them for something they did in the past is not being a loving person.

Forgiveness is a very simple action to take but for some it may be hard to do. Here's a suggestion. Visualize the other person in your mind and say, ***"I forgive you."*** Do this until you feel free of the resentment and hatred of an unforgiving attitude. You will feel good about yourself and your life when you do this. Follow up by continuing to visualize yourself loving this person whom you are forgiving. All the great spiritual teachers, Christ, Mother Teresa, Muhammad and Buddha have urged us to forgive our enemies. These great spiritualists have known that it is good for you to forgive. Not just for the person who is being forgiven but for yourself.

Once in a group organization to which I belong, one of the members of the group criticized me for some comments I had made and some actions I had taken. For several days I thought about how to get even with him for what he had said to me. Suddenly one night, I awakened with a strong feeling that I should not confront him. Instead, I decided to follow the spiritual way and forgive him. So the next time I saw him I thanked him for his criticism. I told him I appreciated his interest in trying to help me. Like magic he smiled and patted me on the back and said he admired a man who could take a suggestion for improving himself without becoming annoyed. Since then we have been good friends. Forgiveness can sometimes work like magic.

12. *She believes she is spiritually joined to others*

The spiritual person believes that she is joined by her spirit with everyone else in the world. She believes that there is a spiritual connection between all people and that we are all attached to the supreme power of the Universe. She believes that God is in all of us. For this reason she treats everyone as she would like to be treated herself. She sends love to everyone regardless of their age, position, wealth or sex.

One of the big differences between the ego and the Higher Self is that the ego believes we are all separate and have no spiritual connection whereas the Higher Self believes that we are all connected.

13. *She believes that the physical body is sacred*

She believes that physical care is vital to spiritual living. Eating the right foods and exercising have top priority. She avoids drinking alcoholic beverages and coffee, tea and cola drinks as much as possible. Her diet is very high in fresh fruits and vegetables, whole wheat bread and grains, supplemented with nuts and seeds, yoghurt, skim milk and skim milk cheese. She goes light on dairy products, meat and fish.

For exercising, she does some stretching and lifting and some general exercises. To keep the heart, lung, blood system working smoothly, she does walking or some striding or running each day for half an hour. For sports, she plays tennis, swims, dances and plays golf. Her philosophy is to use all the muscles and challenge the whole system by walking and moving whenever possible.

The spiritual person knows the physical body is a miracle, which has been given to her at birth, and she has been entrusted with this fantastic gift for life. She knows that if it could be done, the cost to reproduce a human body with all its chemical, mechanical, neurological and emotional make up and its capacity to see, hear, think, taste and feel, would be several billion dollars. This fact alone alerts her to the tremendous practical value of the physical body. This makes her feel proud to have such a marvelous instrument entrusted to her care, and it boosts her self-esteem.

14. *She takes responsibility for the environment*

The spiritual person is concerned about the earth and the environment. She believes it is her duty to keep the earth in good condition and that she must do everything possible to stop pollution and destruction of property. She cleans up after herself and often cleans up after others if they leave debris scattered anywhere. She supports any organizations that are striving to improve the environment. She believes flowers, trees, lakes, rivers and mountains are expressions of the Godliness of the Universe and that she is a part of this environment. The same Godliness that flows through the flowers, trees and plants, flows through her.

Probably the most important difference between the non-spiritual person and the spiritual person is her belief that the power of the Universe is flowing through her at all times. This is her connection to the Universe and God and the great power associated with it. This power and the dedication to love and service is the great strength of the spiritual person. It gives her a purpose in life. Whenever she has any problems or distress she turns to God by constantly repeating this statement ***"Thank you God for always being within me and for bringing the power of the Universe flowing through me."***

I hope I have been able to communicate to you enough about the spiritual attitudes towards life to give you a feeling of what it would be like to believe in the Higher Self. It will bring you a new reality telling you that your connection to God and Universal power is stronger than your connection to things of the world. You may have doubts and you may say "I don't believe it. Many of the things you have told me are coincidences in life. Much of what you have told me I cannot accept."

This is exactly the way I felt three years ago before I read Larry Dossey's book, "*Healing with Prayer.*" In this book, I read about the many validated research studies which prove beyond a doubt that prayer is effective. This caused me to believe there is a God. It also changed my attitude in life from one of winning, achieving and accumulating material things, to one of loving others, serving others, and contributing what I can to the world. The resulting stimulation from these efforts has convinced me that there is a spiritual life, which is very exciting, and we can all have the advantages of the spiritual existence if we will just keep an open mind. It isn't easy and it won't come quickly but it is worth trying to achieve. Don't push it. Don't force it. Don't try to make it happen. Just let it happen.

I am not saying that spiritual people are all right and that worldly people are all wrong. There are many good people who love others and help others who are not spiritual. What I am saying is that the spiritual philosophy is more likely to bring you joy and satisfaction than the worldly philosophy of gaining, competing and achieving.

Here's a story that indicates the power of the spiritual. A very spiritual woman was held at gunpoint one night by a masked man and asked for her money. She reached into her purse, gave him all the money she had and said, "Sorry I haven't more for you. I love you." She was following her spiritual teachings to love everyone unconditionally.

Five years later a man approached her one night and said "Do you remember me?" She replied, "Should I remember you?" "Yes, I held you up one night five years ago and stole your money. Here's your money back. Since I robbed you I was so impressed with your high level behavior that I gave up stealing from people and took up the spiritual life."

SPIRITUALITY AND SUCCESS

Many people in our modern society don't look on spirituality as anything that would contribute to success. They think of it as some vague concept, that is a part of religion which they don't need at the moment because they are too busy struggling to survive and succeed in the rough economic world. What they don't realize is that if they followed spiritual concepts this would be the greatest boost they could get to achieving their worldly goals. Following specific guidelines to a spiritual life might not only enable them to achieve their goals, but to be happy and at peace with themselves and the world.

This doesn't mean that we should take up the spiritual way of living in order to advance ourselves. What it does mean is that if we are living a spiritual life this is not a handicap to achieving our worldly goals. It is just the opposite. Spiritual behavior is the best type of conduct to enable us to get along with others and achieve the outcome we desire.

Here, in this chapter, I am going to describe twelve spiritual concepts that will enable anyone who can follow them to improve the quality of his life and achieve his goals. These spiritual concepts are over and beyond the attitudes and actions of the spiritual person described in the last chapter. Following these principles will help you to move along the path to spiritual fitness and worldly success.

First, let me define what I mean by success. I don't mean men or women who have achieved great power or large amounts of money or great skills in sports or the arts and are often unhappy and dissatisfied with their personal lives. They are known as selfish, abrasive, autocratic or conceited people who take advantage of others, manipulate, and sometimes abuse others physically or psychologically by use of their power or position or money. Their personal lives are often unhappy with divorces, separations or legal actions against them for short cutting the law and being devious in many ways.

Sometimes they are judgmental, critical and unforgiving in their attitudes. These are what I call worldly people who do not believe in a God or a Supreme Being. Not all worldly people are like this, but some of them are.

My definition of success is a man or woman who believes in God or some Supreme Being and leads a life of service and is effective at his work. These spiritual people love themselves and others. They have peace of mind and happiness while contributing to the world and to others in the form of service above self. Here are their approaches to their work that bring them happiness and success.

1. He sets the right goals. Once he establishes his goals the spiritual person concentrates on the process. He keeps working in a relaxed manner with quality and integrity without thinking of his goals, which are in the background. His real goals are to love others and to be of service to all with whom he comes in contact and to contribute something to the world.

You have probably often heard the motivating statement "Winning is everything." The spiritual person doesn't believe that winning is everything. He believes that getting along with people, giving service to others and helping to improve the world, is everything. He is more concerned about having peace of mind and living for the present than achieving his worldly goals.

His happiness comes from his inner mind and not from what happens in the outer world. His attitudes of loving and giving service are what bring him happiness. He can enjoy life and be happy even if he doesn't achieve his worldly goals. You will likely find, when you dedicate yourself to a life of service, all things will be added to you. For example, the motto of Rotarians is ***"Service above self."*** But when Rotarians forget about their selfish interests in the service of others they usually find that ***"He profits most who serves the best."***

Spiritual people have goals not just for achievement but for improving themselves. To do this a spiritual person visualizes the kind of person he wants to be. He develops an image of how he would like to behave in the outer world, helping others and being of service to the community. He keeps visualizing himself in this way and assumes the intention of being this way. Soon he will get suggestions from his subconscious mind telling him what he must do to achieve his goals. If he is willing to follow these suggestions the chances are very high that he will get the outcome he wants. His subconscious mind is all-wise and once he activates it with pictures in his mind it will show him the way to get what he wants.

For example, supposing he is an accountant and wants to become a public speaker, so he can spread the gospel of spirituality. His first step is to visualize himself as a public speaker and have the intention of making beautiful speeches and getting much applause. He holds this picture in his mind constantly, making it large and colorful. Soon he may get the urge to buy a certain book on public speaking. As he reads the book he may get the subtle suggestion that he take a course in public speaking. This may lead to the idea that he should join a public speaking club. If he is willing to follow these suggestions he will probably become an excellent public speaker.

2. He emphasizes the positive. Spiritual people look for the best in everything. They keep asking, "What can we learn from this? What does this mean? How can we benefit from it? Instead of resisting and criticizing they look for what is good in a situation. Spiritual people believe that there is no such thing as failure. They believe a so called failure is just a learning experience so they can gain knowledge and become wiser. Spiritual people believe that overcoming adversities makes them stronger. They look on reverses and discouragements as opportunities to grow and develop.

Supposing for example, the spiritual person is in business and loses one of his best customers. This is a devastating experience but instead of finding fault and complaining he will try to find something good about this. What can he learn? Why did he lose this big account? He could say to himself that everything happens for the best and there is a reason why he lost this customer, which he doesn't understand. This may enable him to replace this large account with several smaller ones that will give his business more stability. Maybe it will cause him to make changes in his business, to move in a different direction and discover new ways of doing things. In other words, he believes that with every lost opportunity a new one appears around the corner.

3. He takes responsibility. Taking responsibility means not blaming someone else for his limitations and mistakes. If a spiritual person isn't getting along with his boss he doesn't criticize or blame the boss. Instead he asks himself, "How can I get along better with him? How can I adjust to him? I must take responsibility." If he doesn't think this way, he is saying that his success depends on his getting the right kind of a boss. If he believes this, he is losing control. His responsibility is to learn how to work with any boss.

So, he will study his boss and visualize himself getting along well with him. Each day before he goes to work he will picture in his mind how well he will get along with him. He will concentrate on anything the boss does well and comment on these things. He will try to understand and like him. If the boss puts him down, he will take it in stride. He will make a list of the boss' best characteristics and keep talking to him about those things.

The spiritual person knows that it's important to keep trying to give the boss what he wants on the job. He should help him to achieve his goals. He isn't concerned because he doesn't understand the boss. He knows that the boss is on his own path. He will ask the boss' opinions and ask for his advice, and thank him for helping. He will keep smiling and expect nothing. If he follows this advice the boss is likely to appreciate him and cooperate with him and try to help him. If this type of behavior on his part doesn't work, he will look for another job with another boss.

4. He isn't defensive. The spiritual person doesn't find it necessary to convince others of his point of view. He doesn't care what others think of him. He isn't upset if people don't agree with what he is saying and he doesn't get emotional or hostile when others openly disagree. Spiritual people believe that if you lose energy defending your point of view you can gain much energy by not doing this. When you defend yourself against others' opinions, you will naturally meet resistance that will intensify and often escalate into a violent quarrel. It can turn a pleasant evening into a small riot.

So he stops being defensive. He doesn't have to be right all the time. Who knows best? Who cares? Does he want to be right and know best or does he want to get along with people? He lets others express their opinions and asks them polite questions about how they feel and why? He may learn something. By keeping open to every point of view, new ideas are going to be presented and he will avoid many confrontations and save himself much energy.

5. He discovers his talents. The spiritual person tries to discover his unique talents and seeks work in the field that will enable him to do what he likes to do. In order to find what these things are, he reviews his life history, in all areas, work, family, sports, the arts, academic, religious, social and social service. He searches his life history to find things he liked doing, did well and felt proud of and tries to make his career in a field that will enable him to do these things. If he can't get into such a career he does those things as hobbies and he will get great satisfaction and stimulation from those activities.

If he can't find the ideal type of employment for himself he doesn't despair. The key to success of the spiritual person is taking any job available and working on it day and night until he masters it. Once he does anything well he will enjoy doing it. So he looks for the ideal job but if he can't find it, he turns on the ideal attitude and masters the job at hand. The result will likely be a happy successful work life for himself. Whatever job he ends up with, the important thing for him, is to focus on helping others in everything he does. It doesn't matter whether he is a carpenter, a day laborer, a professional engineer or a top executive. It isn't necessary for him to be a minister, priest, rabbi, or social worker in order to be helpful. He can slant any type of work so it will be of assistance to others.

6. He has wide interests. By discovering his talents and taking action and performing in different fields, he will improve many things about himself. I have often asked very active busy men and women where they get the energy to do all the things they do. The answer is always that doing many things gives them the energy to do more things. The reason, of course, is that any activity in which they participate successfully will give them eustress, an energizing type of stress. Generally speaking the more things they do well, the more eustress they get and the more energy they have. The spiritual person always has some activity going.

For example, if he plays tennis well this will give him the energy to write an article. If the article is published and successful, the energy from this will enable him to take art lessons and learn how to paint. The energy from this will give him the strength to take up ballroom dancing and be more active socially. This action will give him the energy to work in the interests of the underprivileged. The eustress from helping others will give him the energy to take a course in philosophy, psychology, history or mathematics. You get the picture? Successful activities motivate him and give him the drive he needs to work in the interests of others.

In addition to giving him more energy, a wide range of activities make him more creative, more socially desirable, wiser, and gives him better mental health.

He knows it is important that he keeps monitoring his activities and if he feels pressure or distress, he slows down or eliminates something. On the other hand, if he is worried and distressed with nothing to do, he takes up another activity. He knows that there is more distress in lives with too little activity than in lives with too much activity. The unemployed, the capable housewives, the retired, the people in routine jobs often suffer distress from having nothing to do or a job which fails to challenge them.

7. He doesn't try to be a special person. He remembers that we are all equal. Whenever he tries to prove by achievement, money making, skill development or in any way, that he is better than others, he knows that he is behaving in an unspiritual manner. The spiritual person believes that we are all equal and although he may achieve things and attain material wealth he doesn't flaunt these things and try to show others that he is a superior person who deserves special recognition. If he has wealth, skills or an important position, as a spiritual person he uses these things in the service of others, not to make him feel better than others.

8. He manages his time effectively. He always does the things that are important and doesn't let those things take second place to things that seem urgent. Important things in his life are keeping in good physical, mental and spiritual condition. Any activity that contributes to this is given priority over more trivial things that seem urgent. The spiritual activities in his life such as prayer and meditation are never urgent but they are important and are given priority over things that seem urgent but unimportant, like getting somewhere in twenty minutes instead of half an hour.

He learns to say ***"no"*** to things he would like to do that contribute nothing to his goals and contribute nothing to others. The spiritual person gives priority to helping others and being of service. He fits his other activities behind these things. Can he be more creative and find short cuts to his goals? It's important to be friendly and cooperative and have fun, but could he cut down on over socializing and unnecessary talking. This will save him a lot of time which he can use to help others.

9. He delegates to others. The spiritual person gets satisfaction from helping people to grow. He has no desire to control or dominate others. He shares his position of power with them. This gives him more time to think, organize and to be creative and show initiative. His philosophy is that if anyone on his staff can do what he is doing or be trained to do it, he delegates it to them and gives them the guidance they need to do it well. He does this in all situations. In the family he gives his children responsibility and helps them to learn and grow. In social situations he tries to get others into the act and doesn't dominate or try to keep the spotlight on himself. He has great respect for people and gets much satisfaction from seeing them develop.

10. The Spiritual person keeps developing his skills and increasing his knowledge. He keeps searching for new ideas. He reads widely. He does everything to make himself more efficient. He may take courses in speed reading, time management, stress control, creative thinking, leadership development, mental fitness, physical fitness, public speaking etc. He keeps searching for ways to improve himself, mentally, physically and spiritually. He keeps reading and searching for spiritual guidance. He listens to great spiritual speakers and buys their books. He seeks knowledge that will bring him peace of mind and show him how to be of service to others and the community where he lives.

11. He knows it's never too late. The spiritual person never feels that he is too old. Many of the world's greatest successes came to people in their seventies and eighties. Bertrand Russell, Grandma Moses, George Bernard Shaw, Winston Churchill and many others had careers lasting until they were in their nineties. George Burns, Bette Davis, Bob Hope, Frank Sinatra, Jessica Tandy and many other actors and comedians have performed into there eighties and nineties. So he never stops trying. If he has an idea in which he believes, he sets a goal and visualizes himself achieving it. The older he gets, the more important spirituality is to him because he is getting near the time when he will leave his body and go as a spirit with God into the next life.

12. He persists. If he believes in something and his intuition says it is right and that he can do it, he will keep trying. Success is as much due to determination and application as to great talent. Some have said that your success depends on your ability to take rejection. We have heard many stories of successful people, who have finally made it, when most of us in their situation would have given up. George Bernard Shaw spent ten years of his life writing novels, plays and non fiction works in the library of the British Museum earning only twenty pounds from his writings. However, in his eleventh year he was discovered as an art critic, then as a music and literary critic, then as a great playwright and he went on to win the Nobel Prize and become world famous.

How many great talents have been lost because they gave up just as they were about to achieve results? If the spiritual person believes in something, he will keep plugging. He may be very close to success that might come with one more try. This is particularly true of his desire to become spiritually fit. As he starts on the path to spirituality, he may feel that the presence of God in his life will come easily, but it won't. He will have ups and downs and back sliding in his progress, but he won't quit. He will keep trying. Even when he thinks he is not making progress, he probably is. Slowly but surely he will get the feeling that God is guiding him and loving him.

From these twelve guidelines that spiritual people automatically use in their activities, we can all get ideas that will help us to be more effective and happier.

In making decisions about your work, pray for help and meditate for the answer from God and you will be guided in the right direction. The key to success is to follow the goal of service above self in everything you do. If you follow this course, God will give you the required energy and ability to achieve any outcome you can visualize. If you don't achieve exactly what you want this is God's will. He is running the world. You can try to run it. But if you fail to do it your way, learn to adjust to doing it his way.

Don't forget to be humble and claim no credit for any success you have. Rather give God credit for giving you the energy and intelligence to do what you are doing. You don't need great educational qualifications or powerful experience to succeed. If God is with you and for you nothing can hold you back. It isn't your experience or knowledge that will enable you to achieve your goals but rather your ability to see clearly that you are a spiritual person with the strength of God within you. The very successful people are those who are striving to make the world a better place in which to live and to carry out God's will. Loving others and serving others is the way to peace of mind and success.

LOVE IS THE ANSWER

You can pick up almost any self-help book today and you will get advice that you can cure all your human relations problems by loving others. To me it seems maudlin to go around loving everyone. Especially when they don't tell you what love is. That's the problem I have with this general advice. What is love? We all know that there are several kinds of love. First there is passionate romantic love which has a sexual basis. Then there is motherly love and brotherly love and just simple love that we all have for older people and babies, children and friends. So I think you can see that we must clarify what we mean by love before we advise someone to love everyone.

The experts have many different descriptions of love. Leo Buscaglia, PhD. in his book, *Love* says that love is a learned phenomenon. The perfect love is one that gives everything and expects nothing. M. Scott Peck, M.D. in his book, *The Road Less Traveled* says love is the will to extend yourself for the purpose of encouraging your spiritual growth or another persons spiritual growth. Gerald G. Jampolsky, M.D. and Diane Circirone, in their book *Love is the Answer,* claim that when love is right we don't judge ourselves or others and we don't criticize or find fault. All our thoughts are positive, always gentle and tender. Wayne Dyer, PhD. in his book *Real Magic,* claims that love is giving and has nothing to do with what you receive. It is an inner process. Marianne Williamson, in her book *A Return to Love,* says that love is the oxygen we need to survive. If we hurt our relationships with unloving thoughts we are threatening our emotional survival. Love is looking for the best in people. Joan Borysenko, PhD., in her book, *Guilt is the Teacher, Love is the Lesson,* says that our need for love is the most basic condition for survival. Children whose physical needs are met, but who are not held, and loved, literally stop growing.

My definition is that love is seeing only the good in people; concentrating on a person's strengths and ignoring her weaknesses. I like that. It takes love out of the emotional, passionate field and puts it into the more rational, logical field of behavior. For example when a mother shows love for a newborn baby, she can see nothing but the positive. She can't see anything that the baby could do wrong. When the baby develops to about age one and starts screaming and wakening her in the middle of the night, slobbering and drooling, her love is replaced by a more realistic type of love. This love encompasses all the baby's behavior, including weaknesses, which the mother now recognizes but still loves her baby with unconditional love.

The same rationale applies when two young people fall madly in love. They see only the good things about their partners. They are blind to each other's limitations and shortcomings. When they live together and begin to notice the failures and weaknesses of one another, the magical love relationship changes to something more realistic. George Bernard Shaw has said that romantic love is a form of temporary madness.

What I learn from this, is that the kind of love we want to have for everyone we meet is really a form of positive thinking. It means concentrating on what's good about others and overlooking their limitations. This makes sense to me. If people would stop judging and criticizing others and trying to change them and concentrate on their strengths, instead of their weaknesses, it would be a wonderful world. Wouldn't it be great if we knew that every place we go people would be searching for the good in us and trying to overlook our limitations and accept us as we are? Instead, we find many people looking for our weaknesses and concentrating on those characteristics.

As a general approach to life, this attitude of liking people and searching for their good qualities, is one of the finest beginnings for good human relations and spirituality. If we demonstrate love for others, we learn how to love more deeply. As we criticize and judge others we become fearful of human relationships. Everyone we meet will be our antagonist or our supporter depending on what we demonstrate to them. Generally speaking, if we love others, they will love us. If we dislike others, they will dislike us.

Onc vcry important aspect of love is that it should be unconditional. For example if you are associated with a person who is hostile and critical, you can dislike what that person is doing, but you will love the person who is doing it. In other words no matter what others do, you will love them but you may dislike what they are doing. This is unconditional love.

This applies also to the love of God. At times, you may be

critical of the way the world is operating and blame God for this. What you don't realize is that God is making his decisions based on wider knowledge than yours. There may be past lives and future lives that he is considering. No matter what decisions God makes, the spiritual person gives him unconditional love.

Sometimes you may not understand God's decisions, which are really good for you. For example, Dr. Wayne Dyer in his books claims that the petty tyrants in his life have taught him more than the nice people he has known. He also claims that the adversities he has faced have helped him to develop himself more than the good things that have happened to him. So, God may be teaching us in ways that don't seem favorable to us. Regardless of what God is doing, the spiritual person gives him unconditional love.

Unconditional love also applies to love of yourself. No matter what bad things you think you have done, don't stop loving yourself. You are a perfect spirit from the universe and as such you deserve unconditional love. You will try to correct the bad things.

All the great religions have love as the basis of their teaching. Jesus, Moses, Mother Teresa and Muhammad all taught their followers to love one another and to love themselves as a starting point for being happy. This convinces me. If these great spiritual leaders have found that love is important in their philosophy, I will accept it. They have been students of living, students of people and spiritual students. They have observed their followers in action and they have practised what they preached with great success.

I am going to give you a formula for loving others which

you may find difficult to apply at times, but you will find it works in most cases and will enable you to get along and establish a good relationship with almost everyone with whom you come in contact. Here is the formula.

1. *Visualize yourself getting along perfectly with everyone. If you have been in conflict with some person, start to visualize yourself getting along well. In your mind, see yourself meeting with that person and having a congenial relationship.*

2. *If it is someone you know think about her best qualities. Think of everything she has done right and keep concentrating on those things. If it is someone you don't know concentrate on the good things you have heard about her and ignore the bad.*

3. *Praise her about one of her good qualities or good activities if the opportunity to do this is appropriate.*

4. *Don't criticize her. No matter what she is doing or has done.*

5. *Accept the other person as she is. Don't try to change her. Remember she is on her own track and no matter what she does or says it is her way of behaving. Just let her continue on her own track with you watching in awe but not trying to change her in any way. Give her undoncitional love.*

6. *Listen to her and ask for her opinions and advice.*

7. *Be of service. Give her anything you can and try to help her. Smile at her.*

8. *Expect nothing in return.*

Don't do this to gain advantages for yourself, but rather to help her. Most people will respond favorably to this kind of treatment. I know it will be difficult for you to treat her that way especially if she has been abrasive, demanding or hostile. To help you deal with this I will say that this type of behavior on her part means that she is really fearful and insecure and wants love and understanding. Try to visualize her with her hands out stretched asking for help. She is hurting with a lack of love and instead of asking for love and understanding she is lashing out to get your attention.

Try this formula on anyone you are having conflicts with and I think you will find them changing their attitude towards you when they find you are sending them love instead of criticism.

Some time ago when I was putting this formula together, I had an experience which proved to me how effective it is. One afternoon I went into one of our large retail stores in Toronto to buy a suit. Unfortunately, I picked a man who was the worst salesman I had ever seen. He ignored me from the beginning by continuing to talk to one of his friends while I was waiting. When I asked him where to find a certain type of suit, he pointed vaguely in a direction behind me. After some searching I couldn't find the size or type of suit I wanted. When I returned to him for further instructions, he waved vaguely in the same direction with some impatient mumbled instructions.

Finally, when I found the type of suit I wanted and returned to have it fitted I was feeling extremely critical and judgmental and was planning to report him and have him replaced by someone more suitable for this type of work. At that point, I thought about my new theory of love and decided to try it. I immediately started visualizing myself getting along better with him and I tried to think of something good about him on which I could concentrate. I couldn't think of anything he did right, so I made up something. As I came out of the fitting booth I put my hand on his shoulder, smiled and said, "You're a great salesman. What I liked was that you didn't hover over me or try to pressure me to buy something."

In a flash as if by magic, he changed his whole attitude. He said, "Mr. McQuaig, it's a pleasure to do business with you. Here is my card. When you come in to pick up this suit I want you to ask for me so I can be sure you get prompt service. Meanwhile, I am going to do something for you. Normally this suit won't be ready until next Friday, but I'm going to put it ahead of some others who are waiting so you will get it Tuesday instead of Friday."

I couldn't believe it. My love formula had changed him into a new and effective salesman and I said to myself, "It works." Since then, I have used this method in many situations with great success.

I think we all need to keep reminding ourselves that the greatest needs of people are to feel important and to be understood and loved. If you can give them these things you will get along better with everyone. One of the best things you can do for people is to agree with them. I don't mean by this that you should agree with people when you really disagree with them. What I mean is that being right is very important to all of us. If you tell a person that they are wrong about something, they look on this as a put down and a questioning of their wisdom and intelligence. So, avoid open disagreement with others.

If someone says that they don't believe violence and pornography on TV are harmful to young people, and you violently disagree, try to keep your response under control. Instead of telling this person that they are wrong and questioning their wisdom and judgement you might say, "That's an interesting viewpoint: Why do you believe that these things are not harmful to children?" You have a choice. Do you want to be right or to get along with others and be happy?

Let her talk. You can get your point across in a nice way without telling this person that she is wrong. It's all a matter of tact and diplomacy. Being agreeable with others is vital to getting along with them. Whenever you feel a conflict building up with your partner, instead of trying to prove that you are right you can stop the disagreement by saying "You could be right about that."

This is the basis of psychiatric treatment. What the psychiatrist does is agree with you and tell you that what you are doing is not all that bad. He is trying to improve your self-esteem by not disagreeing. Many marital conflicts could be prevented if the partners would try to agree. We are attracted to those who agree with us. We like social gatherings because people usually agree with us on these occasions. That's why wines and alcoholic beverages are so popular. These drinks tend to bring out the best in people and make them agreeable.

Many experts in marital counseling will tell you that the greatest cause of marital discord is when the partners fight over who is right and who is wrong or who knows best. Marriages often break up because the partners are fighting to prove who is right, when sometimes they are both wrong. I personally think the biggest cause of marital discord is being disagreeable. If you always disagree with your partner, you have a constant conflict on your hands. It can start early when the minister says, "Do you take this woman to be your lawfully wedded wife?" and the bridegroom says to himself, "provided she agrees with me and does what I tell her."

The importance of love and understanding to your health is also demonstrated by something that happened in Rosito, Pennsylvania, a small community which had few heart attacks when compared to adjacent communities.

Rosito had been settled in 1882 by immigrants from southern towns in Italy. These people had close family and friend relationships, which they maintained in Rosito. This gave them an environment filled with love, caring and goodwill towards their friends and neighbors. This congenial setting apparently protected their health. Love is so powerful that it is just as important in keeping people physically healthy as is the right food and exercise.

According to Dr. Dean Ornish, who wrote about this situation in his book, *Love and Survival,* the people in Rosito apparently connected with one another in mind, heart and spirit. Dr. Ornish claims there is a great healing power that comes with connecting, for you and for those with whom you connect. Connecting means spending loving time, having fun together, not sitting in front of TV, eating, shopping or driving somewhere. These latter people are just co-existing, not connecting. They are not really together.

Dr. Paul Pearsoll tells in a Nightingale Conant tape, a story which indicates the importance of connecting. A man who was dying with a heart condition seemed to have no one in the world to connect with. In desperation the doctor asked for some of his friends to come and give him moral support. He had no friends. He had been a difficult man who alienated everyone in his life. The doctor said, "What about his wife. Get her here to console him." The reply was, "No, he never got along with his wife. They fought constantly."

"Bring her in anyway," said the doctor, "Maybe just her presence will do something for him." They brought the wife in and asked her to try and help him to survive. The wife, in a belligerent manner, looked the situation over, then went over to her husband and whispered something in his ear. He immediately gained strength, and aroused out of his coma and his heart began to return to normal. The doctor was amazed and said, "What did you say to him?" "Oh it was nothing," said the wife. I just said, "Harry, if you die I'll kill you."

Apparently a human connection of any kind is helpful to those in distress. Even if the patient had constantly fought with his wife, her presence stimulated him and made a connection that helped. Love has unusual ways of casting its spell on people but a connection with another human being is important to those who are in a low state.

You can solve many of your problems and feel good and be successful and happy if you can love yourself. It seems ridiculous that you are spending time, effort and money to try to achieve happiness and success and yet you could have it all, if you could start loving yourself.

Why will this simple change of attitude make a big difference in your life? Because, if you love yourself unconditionally, you will automatically love others unconditionally. The result will be better human relations, cooperation, friendship and the ability to get along well with people. In other words, you will go through life with less distress and friction and free yourself to use your energy to achieve the maximum productivity.

Why do we have difficulty in loving ourselves? You would think this would come naturally. We are born without any conviction one way or another, but after parents, friends and relatives have criticized us and put us down, we begin to feel that we are not very worthwhile. In addition, the adversities, conflicts and frustrations we face in life often demoralize us and cause us to turn against ourselves. This attitude will not change unless we take some conscious action. The problem is that we don't know why we should change ourselves or how to change.

You can solve most of your problems right now if you can do four things. **First.** Remember that you are really a spirit connected to the Universe. As such you are perfect and any of the weak things you do in this world are offset by your spiritual connection. **Second.** Keep looking for the best in yourself. Concentrate on your best qualities. Always look for the best and emphasize these good characteristics. When you think of yourself, stop emphasizing your weaknesses. Forget your limitations. Search for your good qualities. Talk to yourself about your good characteristics and keep thinking about those qualities all the time. **Thirdly**. Stop blaming and criticizing yourself, regardless of what you say or do. Judging, blaming and criticizing are the causes of most of our human relations problems. **Fourth.** Visualize yourself going through life praising and complimenting yourself for achieving whatever goals you have set for yourself.

Why is criticizing and blaming yourself such a bad thing?

Because if you are judging and criticizing yourself it's a sign that you have low self-esteem and don't think well of yourself. If you don't think well of yourself you will not be happy because you will believe that a "no good" like yourself doesn't deserve to be happy. So you will probably sabotage yourself in some way and destroy your happiness.

With low self-esteem you will not have the success you deserve because you will feel that you are unworthy of assuming responsibility and you will refuse opportunities. With low self-esteem you will be unable to establish a good relationship with someone of the opposite sex, because you think you are "no good." You will therefore be suspicious of any person who would want you and you will watch her and check up on her to the degree that she will probably get fed up with you and break off the relationship.

Why should you love yourself unconditionally no matter how you behave or no matter how little you achieve? Because you are perfect. Yes the real you is perfect. Who is the real you? You are the perfect spirit, which inhabits your body and runs your life. You are the part of you that leaves your body at death. If I were to go to your funeral, your body and mind would still be there, but the perfect spirit that is you has gone. This should alert you to remember that your spirit, which is connecting you with the great power of the universe, is always with you. Keep thinking of your spirit within your body. Remember that your spirit is your direct connection with God and the universe with all the power you need to achieve your goals and be happy. Don't forget that God is within you, bringing the power of the universe into your body and mind.

Who are you anyway? Unfortunately, you don't really know who you are. As Woody Allen said his one regret is that he is not someone else. You may think you are your body. This is untrue because you could lose your arms and legs in a terrible accident and still be there. Or maybe you think you are your wisdom, which is the sum total of your inherited qualities your insight and intuition and your lifetime of experiences. But you are not your wisdom. Your wisdom, is merely the part of you that shows you how to behave. If you have little wisdom you can't help it. Much of your wisdom is in your inherited qualities and you have no control over that.

You might even think you are your personality, but this is not true because you can be quiet and say nothing and still you are there. You might also think that you are your actions but this is not true because you can be still and stop acting and you will still be there. You are not your actions, nor are you your personality. You are the something that acts. So you are back to where you started, you are a perfect spirit, which runs your body and your personality.

The spirit, which you really are, is something which you cannot physically touch or feel. It is unreal in terms of your five senses of seeing, feeling, hearing, tasting or smelling. It is something intangible in terms of the world in which we live. The doctor can weigh you five minutes before you die and five minutes after you die and your weight is the same. The real you, your spirit, was in your body when you were alive and gone from your body when you died. So it is weightless, invisible and intangible.

You are not to blame for anything you have done no matter how bad it was. You couldn't help it. Your limited wisdom prevented you from doing things differently. Blame it on your limited wisdom. This frees you from blame for your past but not for the present and future. You can change your behavior now and start performing better for the future, but you are still responsible for your past. If you did something illegal you have to pay the price. You have to pay the price for anything you do. However you are not to blame. You are faultless because you are a perfect spirit, part of the great Universal Power. So, love yourself for what you are and stop blaming and criticizing yourself.

If this applies to you, then it certainly applies to others. They are not to blame for what they are doing. Stop judging them, criticizing them and blaming them. They are controlled by their limited wisdom and their wisdom is just what it is – the combination of their inherited qualities, their insight and their life experiences.

You are not going to change anyone by criticizing and blaming them. This will just annoy them and cause them to retaliate by criticizing and blaming you. Instead try to eliminate criticism and blame completely. No one needs it anyway because everyone is perfect. Each person is a perfect spirit. The problem is with their wisdom. We all have wisdoms that are less than perfect. This causes our weak performances. So the only way you can change or improve anyone is to change their wisdom, and the only way you can change yourself is to change your wisdom.

So how do you improve your wisdom? First, of course, you should read and study widely in fields that interest you. The more knowledge you have, the more likely you are to be wise. Widening your interests will also improve your wisdom because you will be exposing yourself to more situations from which you can learn. Meet as many wise people as you can. Listen to them and question them when possible to find out what they believe and think.

As you become wiser you will get your wisdom more in alignment with reality. As a result you will behave wisely and your life will become more interesting and exciting.

Love is not only pleasurable and emotionally stimulating. It has been proven in many experiments that it can heal the physical body of sickness. If love was suddenly discovered to have an influence on physical wellness doctors would be prescribing it for all their patients. To begin with it is an inexpensive cure and has no bad side effects, although it is sometimes harder to get than medication. The reason doctors don't recommend it, is because they haven't appreciated what a great curing effect it has. Dr. Larry Dossey in his book, *Healing Words, Harper Collins,* tells about one survey of 10,000 men with heart disease in which those who had understanding, loving wives had 50 percent less chest pains than those who didn't have supportive wives.

The fact that those in love get heart palpitations, blushing, and unlimited energy, indicates the power of love over the body. Tender loving care has always been prescribed for those with disabilities, by those who know the power of love. Recent research is proving that the first kiss a person receives from the opposite sex is so memorable that he or she never forgets it.

David McClelland, PhD, of Harvard Medical School, once told a group of his medical colleagues that being loving to people is good for everybody, both for those who are giving loving care and those who are receiving it. After doing extensive research, McClelland found that he could help people to cure colds by thinking of times when they had been loved by others and times when they had loved others. As a result, he recommended love as a technique in modern healing.

If we accept the fact that we are all tied together in the great universal concept and that we are each connected to one another through spiritual power, this explains why prayers work at a distance. In other words, if you are praying for someone, it doesn't matter whether they are in the same room or one hundred miles away, the prayer is equally effective. The reason is that we are all connected and distance means nothing. This explains why it always feels good to love someone and why praying for someone else is good for the one who is praying. The reason is that when you pray for someone else you are also praying for yourself because you are connected spiritually with that person.

Unfortunately, some who are recommending love as a cure for sickness often go too far and claim that love is the only thing that matters and the sick person can abandon his practical medical help. This is wrong, of course. Love is helpful in healing but all the help you can get from modern medical science is also important. Dr Larry Dossey claims that love should not be enshrined as some magical formula for health and healing. What we can safely say is that love, compassion, and caring help the body to heal itself but it won't necessarily do the job of healing alone. This still leaves love a powerful aid in healing and it is a bond that ties us all together.

Dr. Dean Ornish, a heart surgeon, left heart surgery several years ago to try and find the cause of heart disabilities. In his latest book, *Love and Survival*, Dr. Ornish tells what he has learned about the causes of heart trouble. His findings indicate that isolation from others and feelings of depression and worry are among the causes of heart problems. Dr. Ornish claims that spending time with family and friends is as important to your survival as eating and breathing. Because we are isolated from others much of the time in our modern way of living, we do harm to our hearts and our general health.

One study conducted by Thomas Oxman, of the University of Texas Medical School, asked patients who were undergoing heart surgery two simple questions.

1. *Do you regularly participate in organized social groups?*

2. *Do you get strength and comfort from your religious or spiritual faith?*

Six months after their surgery those who answered "no" to both questions were seven times more likely to have died.

As ways to increase your contacts with others, Dr. Ornish recommends group activity of any kind such as sports, literature, and music, etc. Psychotherapy and counseling can help people to understand themselves better so they can improve their relationship with others. The one on one contact with the counselor is also helpful. Being married, having friends of both sexes and being in love can also strengthen our connections with people. Meditation, prayer and chanting are also helpful. Although these are solitary, isolated activities, they bring us in touch with God.

In our society, loving others and ourselves are highly underrated techniques. Now that you are aware of the tremendous power of love in maintaining your health and well being, you will be more open to showing your appreciation, forgiveness and caring for others.

The great spiritual leaders were right in claiming that all the things they were able to achieve came about because of their love for others.

SERVICE AND SPIRITUALITY

The spiritual person is dedicated to the service of others. He feels that the purpose of life is to help people and contribute as much as possible to the improvement of the world and its people. He believes that he should have the same interest in other peoples' lives as he has in his own. He feels that the most stimulating experiences in life are times when he is reaching out to help someone. He experiences "peace of mind" when he is helping others rather than worrying about his own problems. He has prominently placed in his mind the goal of being helpful to the people who are around him at the moment. He keeps constantly asking himself, "How can I be of service?"

The spiritual person believes that he is a global citizen who has unconditional love for everyone in the world. He has a powerful desire to be concerned about others no matter where they live. Gerald G. Jampolsky & Diane V. Cirincione in their book, *Love is the Answer*, Bantam Books, tell about 60 Attitudinal Healing centres around the world. To these centres come the depressed, the sick and the destitute. These people are changed and uplifted when they put their energy into helping others and being of service.

When we concentrate on extending our love to others and being of service, something dramatic occurs. The spiritual person is no longer concerned about his own problems. In contrast to this, many non spiritual people concentrate on their own problems and may help others when they are not too busy with their own affairs, if they feel the other person deserves help. They believe in the "me first" philosophy.

Some people report that they achieve peace of mind when they become completely absorbed in helping others and dedicate their life to this purpose. Spiritual people believe this and they believe that they were brought into this world to be of service, to try to make the world a better place in which to live. To them, giving is more important than getting. They stop pushing hard for more money, more possessions, more power. Instead they live their lives for the purpose of serving. They know that everything they do is co-ordinated with a super plan to enable them to contribute as much as possible to the world.

Because he thinks of himself as a wonderful combination of body, mind and spirit the spiritual person can project the love he has for himself to others and he will be a giving caring person. His thoughts will also carry this message to others. The only thing he projects to others is what he has within himself. If he hates himself he will hate others: if he loves himself he will love others. All he can give to the outer world is what he thinks in his inner world. When his attitude of mind is that his life is on purpose, and that he is here to serve and give, that will be reflected in his behavior towards people.

When he changes his attitudes from wanting to manipulate and dominate others and from a "what's in it for me" attitude to a giving, helping and accepting attitude, he finds new meaning in his life. Once people see he has a loving attitude towards them, rather than a critical and judging attitude, they will feel positive towards him.

When testing out spiritual ideas while writing this book, I decided to try to act as a spiritual person. One of the ways I did this was to give coins to every homeless person I encountered. When I gave the person a coin he would often smile and thank me and say "God bless you." I always said to myself as I gave a coin, "I love you, God bless you." The result of this behavior was that I felt very good about myself. With some of these homeless people I became friendly and I would stop and talk to them. My approach was always non-judgmental and non-critical.

The important fact to me was that giving was helping me as much as the homeless, by giving me a very good feeling about myself. When you have a problem of any kind, keep asking, "How may I be of service" and you may find a solution to the problem. Keep giving, keep serving. Practice by sending out love to every one you meet, even to strangers and the homeless on the street.

We have always known that giving service to others is stimulating to the giver and good for his motivation and morale. However, we now have scientific proof that this is true. Allan Luks, a social worker has written a book *The Healing Power of Doing Good*, by Allan Luks and Peggy Payne, published in 1992 by Fawcett Book Group in which he describes some research he did in this field.

Luks prepared a seventeen-question survey which he designed with the help of Howard Andres Ph.d., a senior research assistant with the New York State Psychiatric Institute. This confidential anonymous questionnaire was sent to 3,300 volunteers at more than 20 social service organizations throughout the U.S.A. It went to people in all fields where self help was important. Eventually, 3,296 of the surveys were returned and the results were very interesting.

Ninety-five percent of those who returned the questionnaire indicated that helping others on a regular basis made them feel good. They reported increased energy and feelings of euphoria. As they calmed down from the initial stimulation, they were relaxed and felt an increase in their self-esteem. Ninety-five percent of those who filled out the questionnaire felt that their health had improved when they helped others. The more often they helped people the more they benefitted from their altruism. They nearly all said that personal contact with the people they were helping was important to make them feel their best from their helping work.

Unusual as it may seem the helpers reported that they got their best feelings and health improvement from helping strangers. Maybe this was because the help they gave to strangers came from their own desire and initiative, whereas the help they gave to friends or relatives was looked on as a "must do" or a "duty."

When the volunteer had something in common with the person being helped it improved the result from the helping. For example, if a reformed alcoholic helped another alcoholic to cure himself, the reformer got more "good feelings" from this than from helping a blind person. Working through a volunteer organization was helpful. The teamwork approach and the fact that they were helping strangers was an advantage in bringing them the good feelings from assisting others.

If the helper is using his skills, he gets more satisfaction. The ideal would be for a golfer to help another golfer, whose hip was hurt by a faulty golf swing. Putting forth some effort on the part of the helper brings him better results. What these results are telling us is that any kind of helping is good for you, but some kinds of help bring you more advantages than others.

Professor Chuck Wall, who teaches human relations at Bakersfield College in California found a newspaper report which said, "We have another act of senseless violence to report." Professor Wall just changed the word "violence" to "kindness" and created the phrase, "Today, I will commit one act of senseless kindness." He then asked his students to go out and do this. At his next class, he had a group of very excited students who had each done some kind of service. One had given blankets to some homeless people. Another had picked up a stray dog, washed it, cleaned it, and put up posters searching for the owner who gratefully appeared and claimed the dog. One student saw a motorist searching for a parking place and she unselfishly backed out of her parking space and gave it to him.

What impressed Wall was the tremendous impact his slogan had on the students. They were so stimulated that they took up Wall's idea and started a continuing Campaign for Kindness. They had bumper stickers made with the slogan, "Today, I will commit one act of senseless kindness – Will you?" Carl Sparks, Kean County Sheriff ordered 150 stickers for his police patrol cars. The Associated Press ran a story on this project and Wall received letters from all over the U.S.A.

Wall himself is blind, but he doesn't let this interfere with his life of service. He has now copyrighted his "Kindness" phrase and is licensing it to non profit groups. His idea is contagious. One of his students came home one day to find that her children had cleaned up the house. They said it was just a random act of senseless kindness.

Professor Wall's experience indicates to me how exciting it can be to give service. If everyone in the world were doing this, it would not only bring much satisfaction to others, but also to those who are giving the service, and it would make the world a great place in which to live. Wall has written a book on the subject of giving and helping others.

One of the best examples of the satisfaction that comes from giving is the story of a young man whose mother asked him to pick a quart of wild blueberries, which grew near their home. The young man hated to do this, but went reluctantly about the job. Suddenly, he got the bright idea of picking two quarts of berries instead of one. He knew this would make his mother happy and he began to get excited and pushed forward with enthusiasm to pick the extra berries. This is a perfect example of how service above self is stimulating. There is a great satisfaction in doing some extra work that we know will help or please someone.

At Christmas time most people get excited, not about receiving gifts, but about giving them. People will spend many hours trying to find a special gift for a special friend. They get great satisfaction out of knowing the recipient will be happy with this particular present.

Nature is motivating us to help others by rewarding us with good feelings when we do and she is motivating us to love others. Meladie McCarty and Hanoch McCarty have written a book entitled, "*Acts of Kindness,*" published by Health Communications Inc.

In their book, they suggest many acts of kindness for those wishing to practice this technique. They also warn their readers that whatever acts they do, it is important that the acts not harm themselves or the recipient in any way. They also urge their readers to consider the appropriateness of what they plan to do. The authors suggest that acts that are too self-sacrificing may be resented if they lead to obligations. Being careful not to go against the receiver's will is another caution. Be sure what you are doing is what the receiver really wants. Don't embarrass the recipient. Don't let recipients feel that they need your help because they are deprived or low-level in any way.

The McCartys give many specific suggestions for acts of kindness. Here are a few examples:

- Do a simple household task for your mate or your mother or for anyone who is housekeeping. You might leave a note with the completed work, something like this, "I love you and I wanted to do something for you."
- Mail a kindly letter to an old friend.
- Phone someone you haven't talked to for a while and compliment that person for something.
- Visit an elderly person who is sick.

- Catch somebody doing something right and compliment him on his good work.
- Help a stranded person change a tire.
- Give someone a flower from your garden.
- Read something uplifting to a friend.
- Be affectionate to those you love.
- Take someone on a surprise outing.

One of the best examples of how service works in a practical setting is the development and expansion of the service club in the business world. It all started with the Rotary Club of Chicago in 1905. A lonesome lawyer by the name of Paul Harris had come to Chicago from a small town. In order to get to know some people, he organized a small group of men in different types of business. They had no meeting place so they rotated the meetings from one of their offices to another and thus the name Rotary Club. The important thing about the Club was its mission to give service. The slogan of the club was "service above self" and this developed into another slogan, "He profits most who serves the best." The members of the Club socialized and became friendly but the purpose of the Club was to give service to the underprivileged, not to increase business for themselves.

Here are the objectives of Rotary:

1. The development of acquaintance as an opportunity for service

2. High ethical standards in business and the professions. The recognition of the worthiness of all useful occupations and the dignifying by each Rotarian of his occupation as an opportunity to serve society.

3. The application of the ideal of service by every Rotarian to his personal, business and community life.

4. The advancement of international understanding, good will and peace through a world fellowship of business and professional persons united in the ideal of service.

The reason I mention the Rotary organization is because of its tremendous growth and expansion from Chicago to162 countries with more than a million members world wide. There are now 29,268 clubs throughout the world. In addition to Rotary, half a dozen other clubs like Kiwanis, Lions, Kinsmen, etc., have started up and continue to expand. I think the reason is because people keep asking themselves, "What am I contributing to the world? What am I giving?" The service club gives them an opportunity to do something worth while and help their fellow men and women. It makes them feel that they are contributing something to the world.

In cities and towns where service clubs are established, each club usually has some kind of community project. The members of the club work to raise funds for this project and they also get together and do the physical work, which is necessary to put the project over. They work for the sick, the elderly, the people with physical disabilities and for youths who are struggling to survive and establish themselves. In addition, all clubs often band together to take on a world-wide project. The Rotary Clubs recently took on the project of eliminating polio from the world. They raised millions of dollars for this project.

The service club shows how service works in practical situations and how people are motivated to contribute when they feel the satisfaction that comes from giving and being of help to others.

We are all joined together in the world and we can't change the world, but we can change our attitude towards it. What we think in our minds will be projected into the outer world. If we have hate in our minds, this will be noticed in our attitude towards others. If we have love in our minds, this is how we will perform in the outer world.

Loving and giving are the behaviors that will enable us to get along with others and to be happy. These two actions are the basic concepts of spiritual fitness.

PRAYER, MEDITATION, CHANTING, AFFIRMATIONS AND INTUITION

My experience with prayer from the time I was taught to pray in church and Sunday School has been very positive. It relieves tension. You talk to God and get much stress out of your system. You also get a feeling of confidence and strength. You have a hope that God will answer your prayer and give you the things you are asking for. Prayer is therapeutic and no matter how you pray, it is good for your mental and physical health.

In some ways prayer is as effective as visiting a counselor or psychiatrist. These professionals are most successful when they listen and only guide the patient. The good ones do a minimum of talking and advising. They let you appraise yourself by listening to yourself. This type of non directive counseling is usually very effective. Prayer gives you a similar effect. Listening to your prayers and hearing what you want, how you feel and what you are thankful for, gives you a real opportunity to appraise yourself and solve your problems.

Another great advantage of prayer is that you feel as if you have constant company. You don't feel alone. God is always with you. The most spiritual people feel the presence of God all the time. This is very therapeutic. Because when the chips are down and it comes to facing serious illness or death, you are on your own. Friends and relatives can be supportive, but they can't be with you all the time, but God is with you all the time. Praying makes you conscious of His presence. He is with you always because He is right in you. At your innermost center is God and the great connection with universal power.

The important thing in prayer is how you put your heart and soul into it and really concentrate. Turn off the radio and television and try to find a completely quiet place where you are away from the sound of voices or any noise that would distract you. How you pray is a personal choice. Some people must kneel, others use the cross legged position while sitting on the floor. Others pray while they are walking, and others must pray out loud or in a church, temple or synagogue to feel that they are in contact with God. Use any of these methods or a combination of all. Pray whenever you can. Pray constantly. The more you pray, the more you will feel God's presence.

Nearly always in my life I have resorted to prayer when I had a problem or when I needed help with something. Fortunately in my prayers I have always been thankful and have shown appreciation for what God has done for me. In recent years this thankfulness has become a stronger part of my prayers and I have become grateful for all the advantages I have in life. I have also learned to be thankful for all the adversities and problems in my life which have taught me lessons and helped me to think clearly.

I have learned that it is also important to pray when things are going well. At these times you can give thanks and ask for guidance. By doing this you are kept constantly aware of God's presence. If you only pray when you need help or guidance, you tend to lose touch with God when things are going well. This is why many people are kept from the spiritual. They are enjoying life so much and have so much success that they keep thinking, "who needs the spiritual?" So my advice is to pray constantly, no matter how you feel or what your situation in life is. Keep in touch with God. He is the most important companion for you because he is with you all the time, even when you go to bed or go to sleep or when you leave this world.

All my life in praying I believed that it was working. It just seemed natural to me to pray particularly when I needed help and guidance. But I was never sure that prayer was working. I thought it was effective and I felt it was relieving stress but I had no proof that it was really bringing results. Recently when I read the book, *Healing Words,* by Dr. Larry Dossey, published by Harper Collins, I was convinced by the unquestionable evidence that prayer does work. In many cases, described in Dr. Dossey's book under laboratory conditions, it has been proven that prayer does have the power to influence situations and make real changes and sometimes, dramatic changes.

For several years a group called Spindrift (Spindrift, 2407 La Jolla Drive, N.W. Salem, OR 97304) has been doing research on prayer and it's ability to get results. Here are some of the things they have proven by scientific research. First of all, prayer isn't something that goes out to a God figure and then bounces back. We should not pray to God but with God. The reason being, that God is within everyone.

The best prayers are those which ask that, "Thy will be done" Praying that, "Thy will be done" is acknowledging that God knows what he is doing and the person praying should be adjusting to God's way of doing things. The person praying is not asking God to change his ways but to empower him to have the strength to adjust to the world as God is running it. In other words, don't try to order the universe to run your way but adjust to the way the Universe is running. If praying for some sick friend, for example, you could say, "Please God, let your spirit flow through him and give him the strength to survive."

Research into prayer has given us further information. Generally speaking, the more you pray the better the results. Naturally, the quality of prayer is most important but volume helps. Keep praying. The worse conditions are, the more effective the prayers. The more specific you are regarding the object of your prayers, the more effective they will be.

For example, if you are praying for several sick friends, your prayers will be more effective if you call them by name than if you just refer to them as your friends. Experience and training in prayer are helpful. You will get better results as you practice more. Professional coaching from a minister, priest or rabbi could be helpful.

Prayers of gratitude show your appreciation of what God has done for you. Here's a sample prayer. ***"Dear God, I am grateful for all the wonderful things you have given me. Thanks for my family, my home, my friends, my food, your love and understanding and the opportunity you have given***

me to live in a country where there is freedom of speech and freedom to change jobs and move somewhere else if I am so inclined."

There are many things which we are learning from research. For example, when faced with adversity, you should pray constantly. When you are failing at something, call in God to help you. God wants to help, but he needs to be asked by prayers. God will always hear your prayers, so why not pray continually. In your prayers, ask anything according to his will, sometimes his will is different than ours.

Some of us pray according to what we want, instead of what God wants. Devote your life to finding what God wants and follow his will, asking him for the strength to follow it. What God wants is for us to love ourselves, and others, and to give service to others and to contribute something to the world. Do these things and pray for help in doing them, and God will help you.

Praying for others is important. When we first turn to spirituality, we usually pray mostly for ourselves. As we get further along the path to spiritual fitness, we start to pray more for others. God will answer your prayers for others, and at the same time, he will also answer your prayers for yourself. In order to help you, God must hear what you want and prayer is the way to ask him. Remember, there is nothing that God cannot do. No matter what adversity you are facing he can help you solve it.

Here is a short prayer, which I have created. It is brief and can easily be learned by heart. At the same time, it covers all the bases of thanking, asking for forgiveness and for help for yourself and others. It also expresses gratefulness and the desire to do God's will. ***"Dear God, the power of the universe is flowing through me because you are always within me. Thank you God, Please forgive me and help me and help others. I am grateful to you for guiding me and empowering me to surrender and adjust happily to your way of running the universe. Thank you God. I love you God."***

Often we feel that our prayers haven't been answered because we don't get the answer the way we want it. God's ways are different than ours and we should forget about getting exactly what we want. Instead, we may get something that looks different but gives us what we asked for in another form.

There is a story about a man who was caught in a flood which illustrates this. This man's house was in a flooded area and the waters rose so high that he was forced to get up on his roof, in order to survive.

He prayed and asked God to rescue him and settled down to wait for God's action. Meanwhile, two men came by in a canoe and offered to take him off his roof. He said "no" because God would rescue him. Sometime later, two men in a motor boat offered him a lift and again he said "no." Finally, a helicopter hovered overhead to pick him up, but he was so sure God would come for him that he again said "no." Eventually, the waters rose higher and he drowned. When he arrived in heaven he asked God why he hadn't rescued him. God said, "I tried. I sent a canoe, a motor boat and a helicopter to pick you up but you always said 'no'."

Sometimes God gives us a different and better result than we prayed for. The following prayer printed in "*Bits and Pieces*," Economics Press, a monthly booklet, illustrates this point.

A Soldier's Prayer

I asked for strength that I might achieve – I was made weak that I might learn humbly to obey.

I asked for help that I might do greater things – I was given infirmity that I might do better things.

I asked for riches that I might be happy – I was given poverty that I might be wise.

I asked for power that I might have the praise of men – I was given weakness that I might feel the need of God.

I asked for all things that I might enjoy life – I was given life that I might enjoy all things.

I got nothing that I asked for – but everything I had hoped for.

Almost despite myself my unspoken prayers were answered. I am, among all men, most richly blessed.

Meditation

Meditation is an all-important part of the spiritual life. By meditating you can enter the alpha state, which is somewhere between being awake and asleep. The alpha state is also the gateway to your spiritual life. It is the seat of the soul. It brings you access to your human potential. It brings you the knowledge that you are part of the great universe.

Psychologists and philosophers have always said that we have greater capacity and ability than we are using in our day to day life. We are all searching for the way to activate our minds so we can live to our fullest potential. There is no easy way to do this but meditation is one route. The goal of spiritual fitness, which we seek, may seem in real life to be unattainable, but if we keep meditating, we may touch the spiritual power that will enable us to achieve that goal. Meditation is to the mind and spirit like an exercise program is to the body.

Any meditation program has to be adapted to the individual. There is no right technique for everyone and meditation is a constant search for your path to fulfillment and happiness. By bringing you increased relaxation and concentration, meditation helps you to perform more effectively. There are experts in meditation who can show you how to control the mind and do great things with it.

What should happen to you as you meditate is that you should feel stronger and more confident, as if you could go out into the world and be the person you want to be and achieve all of your goals. Sometimes you will get a glowing feeling, which brings joy and happiness into your mind. When you come out of your meditation, you should feel better than before you started. Some experts will tell you that an hour of meditation is more relaxing and refreshing than an hour of sleep.

I am going to describe several types of meditation, which you can experiment with to try to discover which suits you best. What you are trying to achieve is to get into the alpha state. You will know when you attain this goal because you will feel slightly different than when you are awake or asleep. You may feel half asleep or as if you are just about ready to doze off. If you are now meditating successfully, keep with it. This is one of the best routes to spirituality.

Meditation is a way of getting into a relaxed state and relieving tension. Meditation is such a simple technique that many refuse to take it seriously. However, the results of meditation can be quite dramatic in increasing energy and attaining a feeling of well-being and relaxation. Dr. Herbert Benson, M.D., in his book *The Relaxation Response,* suggests that there are four basic requirements to bring on the meditation feeling.

First, you must have a quiet environment without external distractions. Second, you must have some object to dwell upon. This could be a word or a sound being repeated. The third requirement is a passive attitude. You should try to eliminate all thoughts and distractions from your mind. The fourth requirement is a comfortable position. For most of us the best position is probably sitting up straight in a comfortable chair and placing both feet squarely on the ground. Rest your arms on your legs, palms facing downwards. This is to allow the unimpeded flow of energy throughout your body. Make sure you are in a quiet room where you will not be disturbed by noises and other distractions. Don't lie down, or you may fall asleep. You can meditate lying down but it doesn't seem to be as effective for me as when I am sitting up. It may work for you.

To meditate effectively, you should close your eyes, and clear your mind, and try to have a positive attitude. Just allow thoughts to drift in and out of your mind at will but don't think about any problems in your life. Try to keep your mind blank and quiet. Concentrate on your breathing. Allow a feeling of pleasantness and quietness to drift over you. You could have a syllable or word on which to focus. It could be any word. "One" is a good word. Repeat the word over and over, "One, One, One." Concentrate on your breath coming and going. Continue repeating your word and maintaining a passive, peaceful attitude while concentrating on your breathing for 10 or 20 minutes twice a day.

You can do this anytime you feel under stress. Ideally you should do it at the same times each day so you develop the habit. You can also do shorter periods of meditation during the day. Sometimes you will find a meditation lasting five minutes very refreshing.

During meditation, the sympathetic nervous system is not as active as during a waking moment. You may feel calm and at peace with yourself and the world, or happy or ecstatically blissful. You should feel as if you are rising above the day-to-day routine, obligations and duties of life. Meditating twice a day should enable you to cope with life more effectively and have a more relaxed approach to life in general. I meditate whenever I am under pressure, just before a speech or an interview. It refreshes me and enables me to perform at my best.

For many years I used the type of meditation I have just described. I found this method of just closing my eyes and repeating a mantra to be effective. It helped me in many situations to relax. As I experimented with meditation I discovered a more effective method. What I now do is breathe in while I am counting to 4 and breathe out while counting to 4. The counting is my mantra. You could count to 3 in and out, or to 5 , 6 or 7 in and out.

This type of meditation relaxes me completely. I help it by trying to relax my arms and legs and all my body muscles. The result is a clearing of the mind and a washing away of worries and negative thoughts. I control my mind by concentrating on my breathing. I keep my mind on my stomach as I breathe in, and on my chest as I breathe out.

My suggestion to you is to experiment. Try different types of meditation until you find a method that gets you into the alpha state and keeps you there and brings you into contact with God. At first you may not get great result. Keep trying but don't push yourself. It should be a relaxing experience. I am giving you a formula that has worked for me. If you have any problems with meditation, check with a professional. You will find experienced teachers at most Yoga training centres.

Meditation is a situation where God is usually talking to you instead of you talking to God, as you do in prayer. If you meditate once or twice a day, you may open this channel from the great Universal Power. This will give you a way to receive wise communications from the supernatural or from your unconscious mind. On a number of occasions while in this meditative state, I have received suggestions that have helped me to solve practical problems. Meditation connects you with worldly life as well as spiritual life.

In many types of meditation there will be times when you are bored and feel that you are achieving nothing. If you can persist, this boredom may pass and you will find your meditation more satisfying. One effect of meditation is to develop a new way of perceiving the world and relating to it. For most of those who have meditated with satisfaction it has brought them serenity and inner stability, even in the face of adversity.

Although a meditative state will often come easy to some people, for others persistence and discipline are necessary. Often problems and worries will interfere with your concentration. Keep trying to bring your mind back to your mantra and to your breathing.

I have found meditation very helpful when I am worried

about something. If I have a problem that is causing me distress, meditation will usually give me the answer to the problem. If you are worried about something, meditate and the worry may disappear.

In the beginning sometimes meditation may cause you to be unhappy or distressed because it reveals to you a world with a different reality, which is a new way of perceiving things. Until you adjust to this newly conceived reality you may face some distress. Persist and you should eventually reap the benefits of meditation.

As you meditate, various thoughts will keep coming into your mind. I just pretend these thoughts are in a parade on a float and let them pass by. I recognize them, but I don't let them pull me away from my purpose of quieting my mind. The best way to eliminate your thoughts is to concentrate on your stomach breathing in and your chest breathing out.

You can learn much from reading, listening to sermons and educational programs and tapes. Meditation is another way of learning about God and the spiritual path. By tapping in to your inner strength, meditation gives you a new look at spirituality.

When your meditation period is over and you want to come back to your normal state, just count back audibly from five to one, visualizing the numbers in your mind and say out loud, "I am feeling better than before my meditation." You could also rub your hands together and rub your hands over your face as when you are washing. Try to come out of your meditation slowly and in a relaxed manner.

I look forward to my periods of meditation. Because of the relaxing effect and because of the guidance I get. In meditation, you are hearing from God. In the first years of meditating, the biggest advantage to me was the ability to relax or put myself to sleep whenever I wanted to. But in the last few years with my new style of meditation, I feel that I am really in touch with God when I meditate. Meditation brings me many benefits. Research is proving that it strengthens your immune system, improves your heart function and helps your heart to develop the right rhythm. However, the most important advantage to me is the communion with God.

Chanting

Sound has a spiritual impact. Great symphony orchestras, violinists and pianists touch the soul when they play delightful music. Probably the most stimulating sounds come from military parade bands, which excite you and lift you up and arouse your fighting spirit. Jazz bands are equally stimulating in a different way. Romantic music can activate the passions and excite the loving instincts of those who dance or listen.

Sound and repetition are two very powerful stimulants. Chanting has them both. By chanting aloud and repeating your chant, you can move yourself to action. Some one once explained the repetition of chanting by saying, ***"God isn't always listening. So you have to repeat."***

Chanting bridges the gap between body and soul. By chanting prayers or affirmations you can rouse the spiritual feelings in yourself. It's sort of a combination of prayer and meditation. Spiritual masters chant to try and contact the Divine. One saint described chanting as an ancient practise to join the worldly and the spiritual.

Chanting helps to relieve pressure and increase your energy. Sounds of chanting enter the body through the skin and bones and stimulate the nervous system. It is well known that your tone of voice communicates as much as what you say. This reveals the power of sound.

I first became aware of the beneficial effects of sounds and music when I visited a sing along bar in a small hotel. Everyone was singing with all their hearts and it made me want to sing. Each time I visited this sing along bar, I came away feeling stimulated. It was the sound, the repetition and the group effort.

When I started to write this piece on chanting, I felt that maybe I should skip it because I had little real experience with chanting. As I read more about it and thought about my experiences, I realized that I had been working with a form of chanting for nearly fifty years.

In my management seminars, I had a technique for loosening up my audience and relaxing them, which was a form of chanting. Here's how it worked. Often on a Monday morning, I would have forty or fifty grim looking managers who were unhappy at the thought of taking a seminar. To get them in a better mood, I would ask them to stand up, hold their arms up in a 45-degree angle in front of them and look upward. They did this reluctantly. Then I would get them to follow me and jog around the room smiling and chanting. ***"I am happy. I am happy. I am happy."***

The results were like magic. The group now turned from a sullen quiet crowd to a joyful friendly gang. They were relaxed, laughing and talking to one another. The sound and the repetition and the moving around had really loosened them up.

At the time I didn't realize that this was a form of chanting and I used it successfully for many years on groups up to 200.

Although they resisted it at first, they ended up enjoying the laughter and playfulness.

How do you chant? Just say the words in a strong forced manner in a clipped sharp tone with plenty of expression and fairly loud. Repetition is important. The words you use will have an impact and so will the repetition and the sound. You have three elements at work. I understand that most chanters sit down. Others stand. My preference is to move around to try and get the body into the act. I like to raise my hands up in front of me to an angle of 45 degrees and look upward, smiling. Instead of standing still, I like to jog around, which seems to give more impact to the chanting.

My favorite words for a chant are, ***"I am happy, I am happy."*** Another chant I use is to repeat the word, ***"hallelujah, hallelujah."*** Other good sounds for a chant are the syllables aah and aum. Just say, ***"Aah Aum, Aah Aum"*** over and over.

You can also use your name for a chant. There is something magic in your name and chanting it increases your self-esteem. Your prayers and your affirmations also make good chanting material.

To make your chanting effective, focus on your words or phrases and put your heart and voice into it. Punctuate your chant with pauses and make it punchy. You should be presenting it in a voice that sounds like humming, singing and talking combined.

Chanting can be very helpful to keep you on the spiritual path. Keep using your prayers and spiritual affirmations when you chant.

For example, I chant to this prayer, "***Thank you God, I love you God, forgive me God, please help me God and help***

others. I am grateful God." I also chant this affirmation. ***"I am positive, optimistic, enthusiastic and in excellent physical mental and spiritual health."***

The reasons for chanting are to change your mood from sadness to happiness or to change your attitude from worldly thinking to spiritual thinking.

All the great religions of the world have used chanting to help people become spiritually enlightened and connect with the Divine Presence. It is only recently that science has realized that chanting is good for the physical, mental and spiritual health of those who chant. Fortunately chanting is not difficult to learn and each person can develop a technique, which fits his or her temperamental needs.

My feeling is that chanting is as important as prayer and meditation in helping a person to develop spiritual fitness. It gives us another path to God, which we can use when we are walking or jogging. I hope you will keep an open mind and try to learn to chant. It has been very helpful to me in developing spiritual fitness.

For further information on chanting, I recommend that you read the book *Chanting*, by Robert Gass, Broadway Books

Affirmations

Affirmations can be another method of bringing you closer to the Universal Power and giving you strength and help in the day to day problems of living.

Affirmations are positive thoughts on which you concentrate to achieve your goals. Affirmations can change your attitudes and alter your beliefs and get you moving in a positive direction. Affirmations are really positive thoughts in written form. For example, by using this affirmation, ***"God is always within me, loving me, caring for me and guiding me. Thank you God, I love you God,"*** I am able to bring myself into the spiritual orbit and have the belief that God is always with me.

Affirmations can reach into your subconscious mind to get it cooperating with you to achieve your goals. The subconscious is powerful and has a great influence on your behavior and attitudes. It is important to get your subconscious working for you rather than against you. Affirmations will help.

Affirmations can assist you to bring benefits into your life. You can use affirmations to change your attitudes or to change your actions. You can create an affirmation to help you to improve yourself. There are books which will give you suggested affirmations. Two of these are, *Words that Heal*, by Douglas Block, Bantam Books, and ,*What To Say When You Talk To Yourself*, by Shad Helmstetter, Pocket Books.

It is not difficult to create your own affirmations. Keep trying until you get an affirmation that feels just right. To create my affirmation, ***"God is always within me, loving me, caring for me and guiding me. Thank you God, I love you God,"*** took me time and many repetitions until I felt it was just right for me. However, it may not be exactly right for you. Work at it until you find something that fits.

There are a few things to consider about an affirmation if you are going to get the results you want. First, it should be positive. Negative affirmations don't work. For example, if you are trying to reduce your weight, don't make an affirmation to get rid of a certain number of pounds. Rather make the affirmation positive. It could be, ***"I am looking slim and healthy."*** Second, you should always have your affirmations in the present. Don't make it ,*"I am going to look slim and healthy,"* but rather, *"I am looking slim and healthy."*

An important factor to consider in using affirmations is that repetition helps. Keep saying it over and over during the day or when you are going to sleep at night or when you waken in the morning. Can you make it rhyme? Can you say it louder or with feeling? Can you chant it? Can you sing it or can you visualize it happening when you repeat it? These techniques can be helpful in getting an affirmation that works. You can also make your affirmation more effective by including a thank you with it as I have done in the affirmation, ***"God is always within me, loving me, caring for me and guiding me. Thank you God, I love you God."***

Another way to strengthen your affirmation is to write it down. Make copies of it to put in prominent places such as, on your bed or in your car. In this way, you will constantly visualize it. I believe there is an affirmation that will help you with any problem. It may take some work to find it. Keep experimenting. Make changes until you feel comfortable with your affirmation and until you feel it is working. Don't expect magic. Certain attitudes and ideas have been with you a long time. If you have had a bad attitude about something for ten years maybe you should be satisfied to correct it in ten years with the right affirmation. However, I don't think it will be this slow to work. If you aren't getting results try a completely new affirmation.

The best example I can give you of how affirmations work is an experience I had. At one time I was very fearful, afraid of dying, afraid of getting sick, afraid of losing my energy and afraid of practically everything. A friend of mine suggested that I had to get rid of these fears or they would do serious harm to my health. I agreed.

Because of these fears I made up an affirmation, which I repeated constantly in my meditation and chanting sessions. The affirmation was ***"I am brave, I am courageous, I am fearless because God is always with me."***. I kept repeating this affirmation, morning, noon and night. Gradually, my fear disappeared and I became stronger.

Intuition

Do you believe in intuition? Do you ever get a hunch that you should do something or take certain action? Something powerful is pulling you to make a purchase or to call someone on the phone whom you haven't seen for a long time, or to check a certain file at the office. Often when you do get this feeling and act on it, you find that it was the right thing to do. This is your intuition in action. Sometimes it is obviously your intuition. Maybe your intuition enters somewhat into every decision you make.

The spiritual person knows that wise and understanding guidance is always available. It sometimes comes to her through impulses and hunches. These are messages from the spiritual world. The spiritual person respects suggestions that come through intuition and realizes that these ideas are coming from the great Universal Power and therefore she pays close attention. This doesn't mean that the spiritual person follows every suggestion that comes to her through intuition but she investigates it. If she doesn't understand an intuitive urge, she will ask God for help.

Intuition is knowledge that comes to you from spiritual

sources and is beyond the five senses that place limits on your life. The spiritual part of intuition brings you information that doesn't always make sense in the real world. It may give you information regarding danger or risks you are taking or about which things are safe and which aren't. It is the Spiritual Power talking to you.

Here's an example of how intuition brought to my attention something that may help me.

For sometime I had been suffering with a foot disability. I had tried several insoles and nothing seemed to be able to relieve my distress. This was on my mind one night when I went to bed. About 5 a.m. I was aroused from my sleep by a sudden urge to get up and turn on my television set. I rejected this urge because I never watched T.V. in the middle of the night and I was tired.

Intuition or wisdom kept urging me to turn on my T.V., which I finally did. There to my amazement was an advertising program about a pair of insoles which seemed just what I needed to relieve my foot distress.

The information that comes from intuition may be as important to you as food and drink. So pay attention to it. Check it out. Sometimes it knows more than you do but be cautious. If it makes sense when you get the facts about the alternative choices you have in each situation, you can take some action.

Praying, meditating, chanting, affirming and paying attention to your intuition should help you to advance along the path to spiritual fitness.

WHAT'S IT ALL ABOUT

Maybe I am better equipped to write on this topic of spirituality than I realize. There is an old story about a famous university professor who specialized in Buddhist philosophy and was very knowledgeable but he wanted to know more and decided to journey to India to visit with one of the world's top gurus on Buddhist theory. When he was ushered into the presence of the Buddha leader he was nervous and talked excitedly about all the things he liked about Buddhist thinking.

The guru listened to him for a while and then interrupted the professor asking him if he would like a cup of tea. The professor said, "yes," and the guru handed him a cup and began to pour his tea. When the cup was filled, the guru kept right on pouring and the tea over-flowed onto the floor. The professor said, "Stop, you are pouring too much. Why are you doing this?" The guru remarked that the professor's tea cup was filled, as his mind was filled, with Buddhist knowledge." He continued, "When the cup is full it won't hold any more tea and as your mind is filled it won't hold any more knowledge."

The moral of this story is that the person with no knowledge who approaches a subject with an open mind can often learn more than the person who is very knowledgeable. So maybe my lack of preconceived ideas and the fact that I am keen to learn and have an open mind will enable me to adapt to the concept of spirituality.

What most of us don't realize is that our lifetimes cover a very short period. When we are young, we look on seventy or eighty years as an eternity. We feel that the end or death will never come and therefore, we can safely put off even thinking about it. However, when we become senior citizens, life seems to have gone by very quickly and we know that we will soon reach the end of the line. Now we become very interested in the problems of ageing and dying, especially since time seems to be going faster as we get older.

I have lived a full life and when I look back I can't believe how fast time has gone by. My feeling now is that I should have spent more time during my life thinking of the spiritual and preparing myself to face the problems of death and old age. In other words, I feel that death is a part of living and we should consider it right from the beginning of our thinking life. We should be preparing ourselves for the end right from the start. I don't mean by this that death is a bad thing and therefore we need a lot of thinking and planning to get ready for it.

Death may be the best thing that ever happens to us and we should not be fearful of looking forward to it. This is the ideal. If we could include death and spirituality in our forward planning and if we could think of these things as we go forward from day to day in our young lives we would be better prepared to deal with the problems of our senior years.

We would also have more strength, energy, and wisdom to solve the problems we face in the world from day to day.

Sometimes I look out of my office window, which is in the top floor of a 27 story building in Toronto. From there I can see hundreds of people below on the streets all rushing to go someplace or do something. They are all so busy trying to achieve their immediate goals of shopping, going to lunch, visiting the sick, going to movies or rushing to work that they have no time to do any real serious thinking. Life goes merrily or unhappily on and they don't think of old age or retirement until they become senior citizens. Life is so fascinating and pleasurable for some that they don't want it to be disturbed by thinking about spirituality and death.

One of the big questions that eventually faces everyone is what is life all about? Why are we here on earth? Who put us here? Who is in charge? What is going to happen to each of us eventually? Is this life the end or do we go on to a bigger and better life after death? These are some of the questions I will attempt to answer and show you how to adjust to life and enjoy it, to look forward to the end of life in this world and to life in the next world.

To become a happy, spiritually fit person is a challenging assignment. One of the reasons I believe we should think about spirituality from the beginning of our lives is that we can't jump into spirituality quickly. Rather it is something that we have to learn by living and by relaxing, observing, and studying over a period of time. We must think it, breath it and feel it.

At one time there was an eager ambitious young man who wanted to become an expert in the martial arts. In order to speed up his learning time he decided to go to Japan to visit one of the world's foremost authorities in the martial arts. When he arrived at the great man's door and was given an audience he asked how long it would take him to become really skilled in the martial arts. "Ten years," said the guru. "But," said the young man, "Suppose I am willing to apply myself intensely and work twice as hard as all your students, how long would it take me?" "Twenty years," said the guru. "Supposing I am willing to give up hobbies, social life, family activity and sports and work night and day. How long would it take me?" "Thirty years," said the guru.

In complete frustration the young man asked, "Why is it that the harder I am willing to work at this program the more time it will take me to master it." "Because," said the master, "skill in the martial arts is not something you rush at and achieve by extra effort and working under a stressful timetable. It requires a relaxed approach and it has to become part of your life. You have to integrate it into your life, slowly and steadily. If you enter into this program with your eye only on the result, you will not be paying attention to the skills you must acquire slowly." My feeling is that this is also true of spirituality. You don't rush into it and attain the strength and positive feelings it will give you by taking a crash course. You let it happen, rather than make it happen.

I have a friend who calls himself a spiritualist. He has great faith in God. He believes he is being guided by God and that God is with him constantly in his life. On one occasion I asked him if he ever had doubts about his beliefs. His answer was that this does happen to him and he does have to struggle to keep on the spiritual track and renew his beliefs. He claims that the best way to do this is to attend a church or talk with other spiritually oriented people who can advise and counsel him. Reading books on the subject, attending seminars and listening to taped recordings can also help.

Spiritual growth has its ups and downs. Some days you will feel connected with God but on other days you may have doubts. Keep striving. You are probably making progress even when you are unaware of it. Try to have faith and trust in the Higher Power and when in doubt surrender to God and let him show you the way. Don't push it or force it. Just let it happen. Prayer, meditation and chanting will help.

The reason your progress is slow is because you are making a big change. From a non believer to a follower of God is a major undertaking. Take your time. Have faith and try to believe. If you have doubts pretend you believe and keep trying. Look at the joyfulness of others who do believe and remember that God is running things his way, so get on the path to spiritual fitness and try to believe. Adjust to His way of running the world and spiritual faith will grow on you.

I have turned to spirituality partly because I believe there is nothing else in life that lasts or can bring you permanent satisfaction and peace of mind. Life is a struggle to adjust to constant changes and it always will be. What brings this forcefully home to me is the fact that five of my oldest and dearest friends have died in the last four years. These men were all successful in that they were quite wealthy and happily married. Yet when they became sick, the things they had achieved in the outer world, money, skills, knowledge, power and prestige were of little value to them. They became completely dependent on family and friends and God. When the chips were down, the most important thing to them was God. Unfortunately, I believe that these friends had gone through their lives with no faith in God. Whether they came to believe on their deathbeds I don't know, but I believe they had missed much joy and comfort in their lives by not accepting God.

The loss of one of these friends devastated me and caused me great unhappiness. Then I accepted the fact that God was running the world and I must adjust to his way. Thinking this way relieved me of the stress of mourning. The passing of these friends has alerted me to the fact that your health is one of your most important assets in life and God and Spirituality are the only things in life that have any permanence. When you are old and sick you have nothing much left in this world to which to look forward. However, you still have the hope of a better life after death. Spirituality is all important and I think you should always try to believe and have faith.

What this means is that during our lifetime in addition to working on our outer lives of work, family, friends, sports, financial, academic and artistic activities we should also be working on our inner lives of spiritual development. We should be asking ourselves the following questions. What is life all about? Is there life after death and how can we best prepare for it? The ideal is to develop an inner spiritual belief and faith that will help us to achieve the things we want in the outer world, but also prepare us for death and life after death.

One of the best ways to introduce yourself to the spiritual life is to remind yourself that you are not your body, nor your mind, nor your actions, nor your personality. You are a spirit. You have come into this world with a body and a mind but you will eventually leave these parts behind when you die. The real you is a spirit which activates your mind and your body. Without your spirit you couldn't function. This happens when you die. Your spirit leaves your body lifeless, inactive, and cold. Your brain and your body remain in this world and are cremated or buried but the real you, which is your spirit, leaves your body and goes somewhere. Some say to heaven, others say to extinction. There are others who have many theories on where your soul or spirit goes after your body is dead.

If your spirit leaves your body and goes somewhere else at death, isn't this a reason to look forward to death. It is a time when you will leave your body with it's aches and pains and limitations and you will become a spirit with no physical disabilities and with unlimited possibilities. So, at death, your spirit will meet with God and go off to infinite love and happiness. Do you believe this? If not, pretend you believe and it may eliminate the fear of death, which haunts most people. Faith and trust are important here. If you have faith you will be confident and know that God will guide you into eternity.

This kind of thinking may seem like madness to the rational minded practical, worldly person. To overcome this feeling we need to accept a new reality. It calls for thinking in a new dimension and accepting God and the spiritual way of life. Most of us have been too busy to conceive of this as we struggle to survive in the practical world of achievement.

If the real you is a spirit, shouldn't spirituality be the most important thing for you to know about? I think so and that is why I am writing this book. I want to outline a simple formula for activating the spiritual life so you can embrace spirituality, and have the power and strength of the spiritual with you throughout life and until you leave this world.

Death is something we all have to face, sooner or later. There is no way that anyone can avoid it. Some people, however, are reluctant to even consider this possibility. I have done some lecturing to senior citizens to try to help them enjoy their senior years. Whenever someone wants to talk about dying, there are others in the group who shout nervously, "No we don't want to talk about that." There is a definite fear in many people about even thinking of death.

I personally think this is wrong. We come into this world and eventually we will all have to leave this world. Why shouldn't we think about death and what might happen after death? Dying is really a part of living and we should look forward to it rather than fear it.

What is death? Does it mean external bliss or is it just filled with the problems of a long trip around the world. In this Chapter, I will try to explain to you my version of death. Nobody can give us a positive description of what happens after death but many will try. Woody Allen once said, "I have no fear of death, I just don't want to be there when it happens." He also said, "I am not sure if there is an afterlife but I am bringing a change of underwear." At one time, I would have thought that these sayings were sacrilegious, but I now believe that God has a sense of humor and wants us to laugh and have fun.

Dr. Raymond Moody who is an authority on near death experiences (N.D.E.) has listened to the stories of over 2,500 people who have had this experience. In his books, *Life after Life and Reflections on Life after Life,* Bantam Books, Dr. Moody describes many of these N.D.E. experiences. His conclusion after this exercise is that these patients have had an experience of a life beyond this one. In practically every case these people described near death in glowing terms. They were unable to say exactly what happened but they nearly all described it as an exciting stimulating trip making them feel good beyond anything they ever knew in real life. The experience was so exhilarating that most of them didn't want to return to this life.

I went to hear Dr. Raymond Moody speak when he was in Toronto in 1995. My impression of him was very favorable. He seemed to me like a man dedicated to his work, who is seriously trying to find out if there is a life after death and if so, what is it like. So far he has nothing but positive results from those who have had near death experiences and they all faced about the same conditions. They were all feeling great, going into a bright light and having their life experiences run quickly past them. Some of them claim to have met friends and relatives who predeceased them.

Dr. Moody admits that none of his findings will stand up to scientific analysis and that everything he is doing so far is speculative. There is no definite proof of life after death or what it will be like but the scales are balanced in favor of a delightful life with experiences of exhilaration and pleasure. Dr. Moody is research minded, trying to be objective and claiming nothing for his findings. Again my feeling is that we can't be sure of life after death, but one thing his experiences do seem to prove. There is a soul or spirit in every body, which leaves the body at death and goes we know not where.

In one of my seminars for seniors, a mature gentleman in the audience said that he had gone through a near death experience. His doctors had pronounced him dead and left him in the care of a nurse in the operating room. Meanwhile he felt that he left his physical body and flew up in his mind to the ceiling from where he could view the operating room and his body dead on the operating table. He claims that he felt stimulated and excited and had no desire to return to the world. But he did.

Betty J. Eadie in her book, *Embraced by the Light*, Gold Leaf Press, has given a detailed description of her experience in dying and going to heaven where she claims to have had a conversation with angels before coming back to earth. She had the typical N.D.E. of passing through a dark tunnel to heaven where she met the spirits of two of her friends who had died previously. She claims she was shown unconditional love while in heaven.

She said that heaven was a glorious world filled with love and light. There were mountains, gardens and waterfalls. After some time she was sent back to earth because her time to die hadn't come yet. When she came back to earth she was very unhappy and told her experiences to only a few of her close friends. These friends persuaded her to go public with her experiences, which she did by speaking in churches and libraries. This lead to a contact with her publisher and her book was published.

I went to hear Betty Eadie speak when she was in Toronto in 1994. She impressed me as a regular citizen who had this experience of dying. She sounded sincere and honest. I think it would have been very difficult for her to make up these descriptions of what happened to her in heaven. Her experience was entirely positive and she enjoyed her period of death very much.

I can't say that I accept everything of her experience. Maybe some of it was a dream on her part. However she did convince me of one thing. We all have a soul separate and apart from our body. This soul is who we really are. It inhabits our body and operates our body and mind. The soul is indestructible and will live on after the body dies. So death is really a new phase of existence for all of us.

Tom Harpur in his book, *Life after Death,* McClelland & Stewart Inc., says that we cannot be scientific or definite about the conclusion that there is life after death. He suggests it is like a court of law where we weigh the evidence and make a decision. He says that the overwhelming weight of evidence falls on the side that there is life after death, as far as he is concerned and that it is a glorious experience. That's good enough for me. If a Rhodes Scholar who was an Anglican Priest for seven years, and professor of Greek and the New Testament at the University of Toronto and who has interviewed many people with N.D. experiences, feels that there is life after death, I will accept his viewpoint.

What life after death will be like we don't have any definite proof but all the near death experiences of people indicate that it will be a glorious happening with maybe no limitations of time and space and no restrictions that earthly life puts on us. Carl Jung the great psychiatrist, after his near death experience said that, ***"Our imaginations and feelings are inadequate to even approximately describe it."***

Tom Harpur claims that what carries the most weight with him is the clarity and consistency of the stories by those who have a N.D.E. and the fact that many of those having a N.D.E. have been able to change their lives immediately, whereas psychiatry and counseling may take years to make these changes. The experience is apparently so profound that it affects people deeply and causes them to change. While these experiences are not scientifically measurable the response to them is, and the responses are very positive.

Proof that we are really spirits in a body may be found at anybody's funeral. The body is still there and if you had a brain surgeon open the head you would find that the brain is still there. However, something is missing. The body has no life or action. The spirit is gone. The real person has gone. It can be nothing else but the disappearance of the spirit which leaves the body cold and rigid. Where has this spirit gone? It has probably gone to a state similar to that described by those having N.D.E., something which we have always referred to as heaven.

If we could all accept this thinking, when we look at another person we would see beyond their physical appearance and their personality to see their spirit which is the real person. This makes us all equal and all joined to one another as spirits and part of the great Universal Power.

If you find this concept hard to believe, try to pretend that you believe it. As Dr. Wayne Dyer puts it so aptly in his book, *You Will See It When You Believe It.* Belief comes first. Once you believe you will eventually see it happen. So try to feel the power of the universe flowing through you. Get the habit of imagining this powerful presence always in your life. If you can keep this spiritual power flowing with you, it will always give you support in time of trouble and you will always have the great wisdom of the universe available to assist you. Prayer and meditation are powerful techniques, which will help to bring you to God. Chanting and affirmations are also helpful.

It may take you some time to constantly visualize the power of the universe in your body. Keep thinking about it and see yourself going through the world empowered by God. Eventually you will have developed the habit of being aware of this spiritual power within you.

If it doesn't happen maybe you have some other way of constantly keeping in touch with God. It's an individual thing. I had to keep chanting, affirming, meditating and praying to help me get on the path to spiritual fitness but I have further to go to achieve the spiritual strength that I want.

We are all different. I have given you the formula that has helped me. If it doesn't work for you try your own system. What you need is something to keep you constantly in touch with God. Jack Hartman in his book, *Soaring Above the Problems of Life*, tells of how he comes to God constantly by reading the Bible every day and finding quotations which strengthen his faith and give him a belief in God that sustains him under all conditions of the world.

Mary Ann Williamson in her book, *A Return to Love*, explains how she keeps close to God by reading the Bible.

Dr. Wayne Dyer in his book, *Real Magic,* explains how meditation and prayer keep him in constant touch with God.

At the writing of this book I don't feel that I am spiritually fit but that I am on the path to spiritual fitness. Many spiritualists say that nobody ever reaches complete spiritual fitness but many are on the path to it. Some are further along the path than others and some never even get on the path. I accept this thinking and believe that the struggle towards spiritual fitness is what counts. Keep struggling and you will eventually get the great benefits of being conscious of the Higher Self within you.

To help you get the feeling of this spiritual presence and to get you into the habit of constantly thinking about it, I am going to suggest that you use an affirmation which you can say over and over to yourself or repeat out loud. This will help you to get through to your subconscious mind the idea of the spiritual mind. Here again is the affirmation. ***"God is always within me, the power of the universe is flowing through me. The light and love of God are shining down upon me. Thank you God. I love you God."***

Whenever you feel unhappy or depressed repeat this affirmation over and over. If you are under pressure just use a short version. ***"God is always within me. Thank you God. I love you God."*** I also suggest that you repeat it when you are happy and successful. This will keep you aware of the spiritual and will eventually convince your subconscious mind that you are a spiritual person.

A good test of how you want to live is to pretend you have died and your soul, the real you is up in heaven looking back on you and observing how you are living and behaving. This exercise alerts you to some of the foolish things you are doing. As your imaginary soul, looking back on your life, you can see how foolish it is to be trying to achieve wealth, position and power at all costs. What good do these things ultimately do for you?

Of course you need enough money to buy the necessities of life and maybe a few luxuries to help you enjoy your life. But accumulating large amounts of money on the theory that more is better is a useless exercise. If you can tame the ego and learn to appreciate what you have and concentrate on the process of living in a relaxed, ethical, considerate of others manner, you will be much happier. Enjoy your life from moment to moment. Concentrate on the present. Don't worry about gaining power, accumulating wealth and developing great skills. Enjoy what you have.

It's impossible to take anything with you into the next world and there you are rushing, scrambling maybe cutting corners to achieve worldly things, which ultimately mean nothing. Take a more detached approach to life. It will assist you to relax and let God run the world, instead of you trying to run it. It will assist you to develop a better sense of values.

There is nothing wrong with you making money, gaining power and accumulating things, provided you use your wealth and position to help others or improve the world. To use these things for your own selfish purposes means your ego is in control.

Unfortunately, from childhood we are trained to believe that these things are the most important. As a result, we are building our egos and in many cases ignoring our spiritual development.

The only productive thing you can do in life is to contribute something to the betterment of the world and to the people you meet. All you can get out of life is the satisfaction of giving service and helping others. When you look back on your life from the other side of the grave this is the message you are getting.

Probably the ideal guide to living is to decide what you would like to have written on your tombstone when you pass out of this world into the universe.

Another way to set an outcome for yourself is to create the conversation you would like to hear at your funeral. What kind of comments would you like people to make when your life is over. It could go something like this, ***"She was respected by all who knew her," "She contributed much to the world and expected little in return," "She was a valuable citizen," "She supported many worthy causes."*** With this ending in mind you can now go out and lead your life in such a way as to make it all come true.

Now that the studies of Dr. Raymond Moody and Tom Harpur and the experiences of Betty Eadie have given us encouraging information about life after death, we can abandon the fear of dying and concentrate on living a happy and productive life as a spiritual person.

You can do several things to avoid the fear of death. First you can focus on your purpose in life. Concentrate on loving others and helping them and contributing something to the world, which will keep you centered in the present. You can also surrender and have faith in God to bring you happily into the next world. You don't know how it will happen but God will be in control. Trust him to do it in such a way that you will be happy. Visualize that it will happen in your sleep. Up until then imagine that the "light and love" of God will be surrounding you and giving you strength and power.

Think of all the near death experiences of people with nobody complaining that it was a bad experience. Those who have died have enjoyed it. So will you. Spend your last days in pleasant surroundings with your friends and relatives loving them and trying to help them to be happy and enjoy their lives. This love for others is the most important thing in your life. So love and give as much as you can in your final days, and trust in God to guide you and love you in your move into the next world.

LIGHT AND HEALING

A technique for healing mind and body which few people are aware of is the use of "light" in our day to day living. I ask you to keep an open mind about this because it is hard to believe that "light" could have a great influence on your life.

What is "light"? Exactly the simple meaning of the word. It is something bright like the rays of the sun, the moon or the stars, the brilliance of a spot light or an electric light or a fireplace.

We take this powerful force for granted because we experience it every day and it is so common in our lives. Yes, I said a powerful force, because light will make you more positive and will help you to be a stronger, better, person. Albert Einstein in his 'Theory of Relativity' learned that "light" might be a greater influence on our lives than time or space.

If you want to learn more about this force, which is with you constantly, read, *Spiritual Growth*, by Sanaya Roman, H.J. Kramer Inc. I don't have the experience or knowledge of "light" to give you a full description, but I will try.

Just imagine that you are lying on the beach in the sunshine and the sun is pouring "light" down upon you. Try and take this "light" into your system; absorb it. Pretend your spine is an antenna bringing "light" into your body from above and below. Also take "light" into your body through your eyes, nose, ears and mouth and through the pores of your skin. Then push this "light" throughout your body so you will become saturated with "light" in all your extremities and internal organs, hands, feet, stomach, heart, lungs, shoulders and head. This will charge your body with "light," which you can use to sprinkle, shower or spray on any situation or on any people to bring a positive atmosphere wherever you want it.

By just thinking about "light" you can bring it into your system. Take a deep breath and urge "light" to come into your body. Make this "light" whatever color you want. It could be a golden or a bluish white or pure white or whatever color pleases you.

One way to accentuate the growth of "light" in your body is to make a list of all the past times when you have been exposed to strong "light." Just imagine the items on this list to be with you at the moment. Feel and see the "light" coming into your body. This list could include any times you have been in the sun, in a hot tub or swimming pool or just lying or walking on the beach. This list could include playing tennis or golf in the sun, walking to work, shaving under a bright light, looking out your bedroom or living room window at the sunlight. Can't you feel the power of "light" coming into your body?

By constantly thinking of these things you can draw "light" into yourself and fill your body with "light." This will enable you to visualize yourself in all your future activities and social situations charged with "light" to the degree that you have enough "light" to keep you positive, optimistic and enthusiastic and still have enough to give to others.

By giving "light" to others you will establish good relations with them. If you have a social, legal or business situation which is going against you, imagine yourself saturating the situation with "light" and things may eventually turn in your favor. Keep practicing each day, taking the time to brighten up your life situation by bringing "light" into it. Even at times when you are driving, shopping or working, you can stop and bring "light" into your situation for a few minutes.

You can bring more "light" into your life just by thinking about it, and it will come to you immediately. The more "light" you bring into your body, the more strength and energy you will have. There are many situations in which you can use "light" to make your life easier or to make you more effective. For example, if you are taking a trip by plane or ship, you can surround the vehicle with "light" to make your traveling safer.

To protect your possessions while you are away, surround them with light.

At one time I was planning a long flight, for many hours and I was to end up on a cruise ship for ten days. One night I awakened from my sleep very worried about going so many miles from home. I didn't believe I could face the distress of this trip. Supposing I was to have a heart attack or stroke in a foreign country where I didn't speak the language? This worry was accentuated by the fact that several of my friends had been stricken with illness when far from home, which had caused them great distress. One even died from the experience.

As I lay in bed squirming with distress, I decided to imagine myself being engulfed with "light" in my arms, legs, feet, hands, head, shoulders, heart and lungs. To my amazement this relaxed me and gave me confidence. I immediately began to think more positively and very quickly went to sleep. I eventually went on the trip, enjoyed it and arrived home in good health. This magic effect of "light" made me appreciate what a great aid it can be. Ever since that event I have kept trying to bring more "light" into my body and into everything I do. This has been very therapeutic.

To illustrate how this works in a practical way, let me tell you about another experience. One day a friend and I were having a discussion about something which ended up in an argument and some distress for both of us. I left the scene and went about some routine activities. After thinking about this situation for a while, it suddenly struck me that I should try "light." So I reproduced the scene of our conflict in my mind and sprayed it with "light." I also sent "light" from my body to his body. Later when I contacted my friend about something, we communicated with kindness and gentleness, with no hostility or distress from our previous angry discussion.

You may say that was just the normal reaction of two mature people to a situation of conflict. But it was more than that. Something very important to both of us that ended up in considerable distress was corrected dramatically and immediately with no hangover effect. I believe "light" improves human attitudes and behavior.

You can immerse yourself in "light" by putting a blanket of "light" around yourself. Wrap the blanket over your head and your feet. This feeling of being surrounded by "light" will bring you energy and vitality. After doing this, you will be able to keep calm and relaxed and be more cordial and understanding. In any business or social situation you can improve relationships by wrapping yourself in "light" and encircling all those present with "light." Being wrapped in "light" will also protect you from hostile remarks and disparaging attitudes.

By bringing "light" into your life, you will feel that the universe is a friendly place, trying to help you rather than harm you. Regardless of what's happening in your environment "light" can make things easier for you.

"Light" should help you to control the future. When you are visualizing what you want your future to be, add "light" to the picture and it will enhance your positive approach.

"Light" is also a powerful influence in curing physical disabilities. If you have pain or a feeling of weakness in your body, try sending "light" to that area. Surround the area and focus it with all the "light" you can generate and you may find your disability changing and your pain subsiding.

As you practice using "light" on yourself and sending it out to other people or to different situations, you will become more skilled in the use of "light" and able to benefit more and more from it's use.

In addition to the therapeutic effects of "light," "color" is also a positive influence in your life. In his book, *Light, Medicine of the Future,* Jacob Liberman, Bear & Co. Publishing, has collected the results of dozens of research studies into the effect of "light" on the human mind and body. These studies have all proven that "light" and "color" can bring a strong positive influence into your life.

One of the exercises, which Dr. Liberman describes, is to imagine a strong beam of white "light" coming into your head. When it reaches your neck, imagine this beam of light breaking out into the colors of red, orange, yellow, green, blue, indigo and violet. Imagine these colors going into all parts of your body. The result will usually be a stabilizing of your body and a positive feeling towards yourself.

Using "light" and "color" to change your mood and attitude may seem like a ridiculous exercise but try to keep an open mind. If you want the results of large numbers of research studies, which prove that "light" and "color" are powerful stimulants, read Dr. Liberman's book.

If you are serious about using "light" in your life you should also read David Cousins book, *Handbook for Light Workers*, Barton House, Dartmouth, England. He gives many exercises and examples of how light can be used to improve your life. One of his exercises which has helped me is the following:

Sit up in a chair or lie in a bed with your body straight. Breathe in to the count of seven and breathe out to the count of seven. Now bring "light" down through the top of your head and concentrate it in your heart area, from which it will spread to all parts of your body. Now imagine bringing black healing energy up from the earth throughout your entire body. Imagine that any physical disability in your body is covered by an ice cube. Let the black healing energy from the earth melt the ice cube covering your physical disability and cure it. Then bring white light down into your body through the top of your head. Let this energy push the black energy out of your body into your surrounding aura.

Repeat this exercise at least three times and you may melt the ice cube and cure your disability. Once you get experience with this exercise you can do it in a few seconds. This will enable you to do it anytime during the day when you have a few minutes to spare. It may eventually help to heal your body and give you better health depending on how skilled you are as a "light" user. I believe this exercise works on your subconscious mind to get it to take action to cure your disability.

I urge you again to keep an open mind on the subject of "light." It is hard to believe that something so prevalent in our lives can be so helpful. To make you realize how important "light" is try moving around in the dark.

Some philosophers and psychologists believe that it is possible to cure yourself of physical disabilities by controlling your mind and the thinking processes. The theory behind this concept is that the spirit within you or the mind of God, which is flowing through you, controls your physical body. The mind and the body are closely connected and whatever the mind thinks or feels is transferred immediately to the body. The subconscious mind is powerful and if you can activate it you may cure what ails you.

For example, if you are experiencing stressful situations in your life you may notice heavy tension in the nerves of your stomach. Your nerves are connected to your muscles and tendons and therefore any tension in the nervous system is translated into physical action and will cause physical distress in the stomach area and eventually in other parts of the body.

To offset any stressful situation, which is causing you

physical disability you should take some actions, to correct this situation. I am going to give you fifty methods of physical, mental and spiritual health improvement, which should help you to keep in good condition and prevent your ego from influencing you in a negative way.

1. Think of God being within you always, bringing the power of the universe into your mind and body and healing you of all disabilities. Remember, that you are really a spirit from the Universe. This spiritual strength can help to make you healthy. Think of the spirit within you, which has perfect health trying to bring perfect health into your physical body. Just imagine that your body is healthy and free of disease and addiction.

   Unfortunately, our modern society has been concerned mostly with our physical and mental health and has neglected the spiritual. This is partly because we are struggling so hard to succeed in the practical world of money-making and achieving, that we are completely absorbed in these outer activities. What we have failed to realize is that without spiritual support in our lives, we are likely to be discontented and unhappy.

2. You can often solve your problems and improve your mental health by flying out of your body and observing yourself in action. Remember you are a spirit from the universe, so you can become the observer by getting out of your physical body and observing yourself performing in the physical world. This action will give you a more objective view of your behavior and will take some of the emotion out of what you are doing. This will enable you

to be more rational about your problems and be more effective in solving them. It will help you to stop worrying and start trying to change whatever is bothering you.

3. Positive thinking and visualizing will carry a strong message from your nerves to the stomach and all parts of your body. Have a mental list of positive things to think about. Whenever your ego picks up a negative thought, swish it away and substitute a positive thought. Visualize yourself achieving your goals and intending to have excellent physical mental and spiritual health as you go through life. Have faith that this will happen. Be positive. Optimists live longer than pessimists. Be optimistic about the future. Keep trying new and different things, which will be stimulating and exciting. Keep learning as you grow older and keep interested in everything.

4. Your beliefs are a powerful influence on your health. If you believe you will be healthy the chances are good that you will be healthy. So expose yourself to positive writing on health and to people who are positive. Try to get a doctor who believes you have great control over your health by food and beverage choices, exercising and life style adjustment. You can also consult with a naturopathic doctor, who can advise you how to lead a life eating natural foods, herbs and hormones and getting plenty of exercise. In addition to this, you can consult with a chiropractor, and experts in massage, shiatsu, acupuncture and mental health.

Believe, that by concentrating on your health and working at it, you can maintain your good physical, mental and spiritual condition, as you grow older. If you want further information on how to do this, read Shad Helmstetter's book, *Finding the Fountain of Youth Inside Yourself*, Pocket Books and Deepak Shopra's book, *Ageless Body, Timeless Mind*, Harmony Books.

Be careful of falling into the trap of deliberately getting sick in order to get attention. Work to get attention for being exceptionally healthy, rather than for being sick.

5. Be flexible in your ideas. Don't become rigid and fixed on one point of view. Be creative and open to new ways of thinking and behaving. Keep up to date by reading newspapers and magazines and by watching for different activities and different concepts on radio, television and the computer. Some Christian Scientists have proven that they can cure themselves of incurable diseases by eliminating disease from their thinking. If you need help to interpret this message, go to the nearest Christian Science Reading Room and someone will guide you. Nearly every city has one of these rooms.

6. You can use chanting to improve your health. Try this for a chant, ***"I am in excellent physical mental and spiritual health."*** Repeating this out loud while you are jogging around gently will have a powerful impact. You will be getting the mind, the body and the sound influencing your subconscious mind. You can also chant your prayers and other affirmations.

7. Smiling and laughing are certainly strong positive thrusts that will help to turn around any negative direction that

your body may be taking. If you can't generate a real laugh use a fake laugh ***"ha ha ha" "ha ha ha."*** Bring as much humor into your life as possible. Search for situations, which are funny and try to expand them. Be mischievous at times. Laugh at your own weaknesses and limitations. If you are on the path to spiritual fitness you will be happy and joyful. Try to expand this feeling as much as possible.

Probably our best example of how effective laughter can be in the health area comes from Norman Cousins, author of *Anatomy of an Illness*. In his book Norman Cousins describes how he helped cure himself of an apparently incurable disease by laughing.

He arranged to get reruns of the old television show "Candid Camera" and some old Marx Brothers movies. He also had his nurses read him humorous books. Slowly his health improved and after sometime he cured himself.

8. Words in the form of affirmations have a great impact on the nervous system and will carry a message to your subconscious mind and body. The words could be an affirmation like this; ***"My nerves can carry a message from Universal Intelligence to all parts of my body which will bring me excellent physical and mental health."*** An alternative affirmation could be ***"I am bringing the power of God into my mind and body to use the creative intelligence of the universe to help me keep in good physical and mental condition."***

9. Your job is vital to your health because you spend eight hours a day in that situation. Try to get into a field of

work that you love and into an organization where you can be happy. If you enjoy your work and do it well you will get satisfaction from achievement which will stimulate your mind and body and improve your health. Your job will also give you a purpose for living.

To discover what your work should be, study your history of activities in the family, social, hobby, economic, sports and work areas. What things have you liked doing, done well and felt good about? Get your job and hobbies in these areas as much as possible. Try to be very good at your work. Master your job so you will get the thrill of achievement. Slant all your activities in your job as much as possible to show unconditional love for others and to improving the world. This will give you a big purpose to live for.

Always keep working at your job. Never retire, just slow down. If you must retire from your life's work, get some other activity going so you will always have a purpose in life. This is one of the most important things to keep you living a long and healthy life. Be sure to take a break from your job each year. You should have at least two weeks vacation.

Traveling is helpful in giving you a break away from your job because it gets you into a different situation. When traveling, you forget your work problems temporarily. You are so occupied with arranging your hotel accommodations and your eating and entertainment activities that you forget about any bigger worries you have. Don't expect traveling to clear up all your difficulties, but it will give you temporary relief and an opportunity to look at your problems from a different direction.

Start right now to get into the type of work you like. If you are a bookkeeper and want to be a personnel counsellor, get a part time job doing personnel work on weekends or at night. Don't give up your present job until you are fairly well established in your new work.

You will do better work if you love what you are doing. You will be a stronger person, contributing more to society, if you are doing what you like. In a way it's your duty to get into the right job.

10. Deep breathing can carry oxygen into your body which will keep you in a healthy state. Breathe in to a count of seven, and breathe out to a count of seven, whenever you feel any stress or pressure.

11. Think about someone you love. Imagine you are touching and hugging him or her. This will bring a positive reaction into your body which will stimulate your nerves to make your body healthy. Try to live with someone so you won't be spending too much time alone. Select a person who is spiritually fit! Remember your very survival depends on your contacts with others.

    If you live alone and don't have friends or relatives to visit you, pray and meditate and bring God into your life so you enjoy the constant companionship of God. If you can be with God all the time and feel close to him, you will find peace of mind and happiness while living alone. Some people are not socially oriented and may want to live alone.

12. Love yourself. You are a perfect spirit from the Universe and your purpose on earth is to love yourself and others

and to contribute something to the world. Remember that you are a great person, deserving the best the world has to offer. God is within you and God created you, so you are the best.

13. Relax and get into a good physical state. Practice progressive relaxation to get all your body parts into a calm condition. Schedule your activities loosely so if you feel under pressure you can cancel something. Make sure you are getting adequate rest and sleep. Somewhere between six and eight hours per day should be enough.

    Maybe you can split your sleeping into two sessions. By sleeping in the afternoon you will need less sleep at night and you will need a total of less sleep. An afternoon sleep will keep you from getting fatigued in the day time. Sir Winston Churchill proved that an afternoon sleep improved his effectiveness when he was under war time pressure.

    Other methods of relaxing are meditation, praying, chanting and deep breathing.

    Turning to God and surrendering your problems to him will free you of stress and worry and help you to relax. Don't work too hard and don't take responsibility too seriously.

    Remember it's a game and being relaxed and creative is more important than working hard under pressure. Keep your temper under control and keep calm.

    Visualize yourself being a relaxed person with trust in God. Keep trying different methods until you get the habit of being relaxed as you go about your daily routine.

Stop rushing and striving. Concentrate and have the intention of being relaxed and patient. Forget about your goal, just work to a standard of excellence in whatever you are doing and you will achieve the results you want.

Remember that relaxation and patience, soon bring results. This is because when you are relaxed and patient in doing your work, it indicates that you have faith in God to help you achieve your goals. He will help you and you will get the results you want if you can be patient and get into the relaxed pace of the world as God is operating it.

14. Concentrate on the present. Try to forget the past and the future and put all your energy into thinking of the present. Concentrate on your breath coming and going. Let other thoughts pass out of your mind. Feel the energy from the Universe flowing into your body and healing it. Constantly think of the "light" of God shining down upon you and the power of God flowing through you. These thoughts will help to keep you in the present. Just knowing that concentrating on the present is important will help you to keep present oriented.

15. Be generous. The world is a very prosperous place. It has plenty of everything. Keep it moving. If you are stingy and hoard things you kill the momentum of prosperity. When in doubt about what to give as a tip or to charity, always give the larger amount.

    Give away things you aren't using. If you haven't worn a particular piece of clothing for two years, give it away. Go through your wardrobe and clean it out.

16. Be grateful. Look at all the things you have. A great body and mind, a home, a car, a job, food to eat, an opportunity to rest and participate in the pleasures of music, reading, writing, art and dancing. You also have the advantage of living in a free country where you can say what you want, change jobs when you want and move around when you want. Be thankful for your job and the purpose you have in life of helping others and contributing to a better world.

17. Pray. Prayer has been proven to have the power to cure. Pray for excellent health. Constantly thank God for all he has given you. Pray for others. Ask God to give them peace of mind and happiness. Ask God to keep guiding you, empowering you and helping you to turn over problems you can't solve, to him.

18. Meditate. Meditation is God talking to you. Listen to God's messages. These messages will give you positive suggestions, which will help heal your body and keep it in good condition. Meditation will relax you and help you to stop rushing and it will synchronize your activities with the pace of the world. Meditate half an hour in the morning and half an hour in the evening, if possible. In chapter 6 you have information on how to meditate.

    Keep thinking of the great benefits of meditation. In addition to relaxing you and helping you to rise above the stress and pressures of daily life it strengthens your immune system to help keep you free of colds, flu and pneumonia. It also strengthens your heart, lung, blood delivery system, which will defend you against heart attacks and strokes. It strengthens your inner organs; liver, heart kidneys, lungs, etc., to keep them healthy.

19. Surrender. Think of being guided by God. Let God take over and cure your body of everything. Just imagine God being throughout your system bringing you excellent physical and mental health. Surrender all your health problems to God and stop worrying.

20. Bring "light and love" into your body and spray it throughout your system. Charge your body with "light and love." Then you will have "light and love" available to spray on situations where you want to establish good human relations, which will be a positive influence on your health. You can also spray "light and love" on any physical disability which is causing you distress.

    Get some sunlight as often as possible but be sure to use protection from the harmful rays. Imagine the "light and love" of God shining down upon you and bringing you the love of God and the power of the universe as you go about your daily routine. Imagine the light and love of God collaborating with your subconscious and your subconscious parts to make you positive, optimistic and enthusiastic.

21. Exercise your heart, lung, blood delivery system by actively moving around. This will stimulate and strengthen your heart. Sports are one of the best ways to exercise. Tennis, golf, cycling, swimming, bowling, jogging or walking are all beneficial. Also do some lifting, pushing and stretching to exercise your muscles. Try to do half an hour of fairly strenuous exercises every day.

The research to-day is showing that walking is one of the best forms of exercising. Take every chance you get to walk. If you can't walk all the way to your job, at least walk part way. Park your car a distance from where you work and walk the rest of the way. Look for opportunities to walk. Some people can walk while they read. One thing we can all do is walk up and down the room while watching television. Walk while waiting for a bus, train or aeroplane. Keep moving and keep healthy.

22. Take some action towards helping someone with a problem. Helping others will remove your mind from your own problems and you will be positively stimulated. If you want to be happy try to make others happy.

23. The food you eat and the fluids you drink all nourish your body and strengthen it so it can cure physical disability. Eat mostly fresh fruits and vegetables and whole grain cereals or breads, with a little fish and chicken. Cut down on sugar. Green tea, which the Chinese have used for many years, is a very therapeutic fluid. Apple cider vinegar and cranberry juice are other fluids which will contribute to your health. Water is vital to your long-term survival. Some doctors recommend 8 glasses per day.

    Eat natural foods as much as possible. Eat light meals. Eat breakfast every day. Other foods which are healthful for most people include, sunflower seeds, pumpkin seeds, sesame seeds, almonds, yoghurt, wheat germ, oat bran, lecithin, black strap molasses, honey and whole grains.

    Watch for new knowledge in the health area. Research in this field is increasing. For example there are two concepts of health which you should explore. One concept is that tablets and fluids, containing the essence of seaweed, can bring vitamins and minerals into your diet. The other concept is that tablets and fluids, containing the essence of many dried fruits and many dried vegetables, can bring essential minerals and vitamins into your diet.

Keep reading and listening to new health information on radio and T.V. Only follow advice that makes sense to you and which has been proven by research and which is as natural as possible. Eliminate smoking and take a maximum of two alcoholic drinks each day and only two drinks of caffeine beverages, tea, coffee and cola. Eliminate alcohol and caffeine drinks completely if possible. If you are addicted to tobacco, alcohol or drugs, pray for help. Alcoholics anonymous has proven that faith in God is the way to cure yourself of addictions.

24. Vitamins can help to bring into your body elements that are lacking in the foods you eat. Get professional advice on what you need. This advise is available in many drug stores. Herbs can also be a positive influence on your body and can help to keep you in excellent health.

25. Hormone replacement can improve your health. Consult with a medical doctor or a naturopathic doctor regarding hormone replacement therapy. Hormone deficiency can occur in your body, as you grow older.

26. Try to be child like in your behavior. Be capable of getting down on the floor and playing with children. Read them stories. Play active games such as hide and seek

and tag. Enjoy letting go of your inhibitions and be a child again.

27. Widen your interests. Each activity in which you participate successfully will bring you satisfaction from achievement. Many activities will bring you a synergistic affect and make you feel good. This will bring positive action to your nervous system and contribute to your good health. Try as much as possible to slant all your activities to loving people, helping them and contributing something to the world.

    Keep an open mind and remember that you can learn something from everyone. Your parents, your brothers and sisters, your children and your friends, neighbours and associates have something to teach you. Listen and observe as you go through life and you can learn something from everyone.

28. Can you play a musical instrument or dance, or sing, paint or write? Any of these activities will stimulate your nervous system in a positive way.

29. You are part of the great universal environment. Remember that God is within you and everyone else and within all the plants and animals. You are part of the same universal system. Commune with nature as much as possible. Walk in the woods and look at the trees and flowers and shrubs. God is within them all. Admire the mountains, rivers, lakes and oceans.

30. Meet with your family or close friends in exciting social events. This will stimulate your positive feelings. Dr.

Dean Ornish has led the way in proving that living in a loving, caring environment is necessary to good health. He spells it all out clearly in his book *Love and Survival*, Harper Collins. In this book he describes some of the research that has been done in this area.

From this research he concludes that anything that creates a sense of love, intimacy, connection and community is healing. He claims that having a loving environment in your life is more important than the right exercise or diet, more important than giving up smoking, more important than the right surgery or having the right genes. Your very survival depends on the congenial contacts you have with others. One of the interesting findings of Dr. Ornish's research was that the person who gives love, benefits as much as the person who receives love.

For example, if you tell someone you love them, you benefit as much as the person whom you are loving. So tell everyone you love them, wherever it is appropriate. You can expand this idea to help you even when you are alone. Just think about God and say to yourself, ***"I love you God, I love you God."*** This should give you some of the positive effect that you would get from a person to person contact, where you tell someone you love them.

31. The spiritual person doesn't have to do things perfectly. He realizes that trying for perfection is very stressful and it is impossible to reach. He knows that his goal is not to achieve perfection in the things he does but to do them well and enjoy what he does. Unfortunately we have been taught to try to be perfect in everything we do and some-

times we avoid things because we don't think we can do them perfectly. As human beings we weren't designed to be perfect. It is more important to get things done well. Trying to be perfect can slow you down and cause indecision and in the long run prevent you from achieving your goals. Even the most capable people make mistakes and sometimes fail to do things just right.

The spiritual person knows he doesn't have to prove himself by doing things perfectly and he settles for doing things in the best way possible for him.

32. You can use your wisdom to help you with specific problems. You have within you a wise being – let's call her Wisdom. Visualize what this person is like. This is really your "gut feeling" that you are talking to. Ask questions of Wisdom. Request whatever you want from her. You should soon get an answer.

If you don't get an answer, forget it and go about your daily duties. You may get the answer later from a story or from someone else, or from something that happens to you.

Wisdom knows what is right for you. Wisdom will guide you if you trust her.

Unfortunately sometimes very intelligent people have little wisdom. Your intelligence is a matter of your thinking whereas wisdom deals with both your thinking and your feeling. If you have a problem which has caused you to do a lot of heavy thinking, try to get your mind quiet through meditation, then step back from your problem. At this point Wisdom may give you an answer, which you will feel is just right. It has a spiritual feeling. This doesn't mean that you should accept every solution that Wisdom suggests. Before acting on it, subject it to critical analysis.

It takes practice to hear and trust Wisdom. Be honest and always tell the truth and Wisdom will help you.

33. Avoid conflicts. Try to be agreeable with people. Don't always have to be right or to know best. Listen to people and try to agree with what they are saying. Instead of arguing, apparently agree by saying ***"You could be right about that."*** Don't try to control or dominate others.

34. Get control of your life through affirmations and visualizing the way you want your life to be. You have more control than you think. You become close to what you think about all day long and what you visualize and what you intend. Figure out the ideal life which will make you happy and visualize it happening and intend it to happen. You are controlled to a large degree by the pictures in your mind, so create pictures of the ideal life for yourself. Make those pictures colorful, large and dynamic and intend to make them happen. Do the best you can to control your life. Whenever it doesn't work out the way you plan it, accept God's will and adjust to his way.

35. Manage your money wisely and live within your means. This can be a real challenge to you. Investing some money in the stock market has its risks but it can be an exciting activity. However be careful and get good advice before you do any speculating, and only speculate with money you can afford to lose. Keep the bulk of your money in G.I.C.'s, blue chip stocks and bonds. Managing your

money wisely is a life study but it can be an interesting and challenging activity.

36. If someone hurts you, be honest. Tell him or her why it hurts. Express your feelings by saying, ***"I feel badly when you say that,"*** or "***My feelings are hurt by that***" Don't be critical. Forgive and show unconditional love. You can protect yourself from the hostilities of others by wrapping yourself in a blanket of light and spraying light on the situation. Fly up above your body. You are a spirit within your body and you can leave it when you want. By observing yourself in action from above you will reduce the pressure. Remember that you are in this world but not of this world. You can withdraw from any worldly conflict in which you are involved and be the observer. Think these thoughts and take these actions and you will be less vulnerable to conflicts and hostilities.

    You could also repeat an affirmation which will help you in situations where you are the object of hostility or criticism. Here is a sample affirmation which you might keep repeating "***I am strong, positive and optimistic, capable of enduring criticisms, complaints, disagreements and conflicts.***"

37. Simplify. Do everything you can to make life simpler. For example, you might go through your wardrobe and personal possessions and give away anythings that you aren't using regularly. Avoid making commitments that call for time appointments. You need personal contact with people but keep control of your time by being free to avoid any activities, when you feel so inclined. Simplify

your finances by concentrating your investments. You need diversity but if you have 10 blue chip stocks. You might cut them down to 5. Strive for simplicity in everything you do.

38. If fear is dominating your life don't hide from it. Face it. Give it a name. I just call it by its real name, Fear. Acknowledging Fear is half the problem. It may be telling you something. Breathe deeply when you are afraid of something. Talk to your Fear. Ask it what it's trying to tell you. Listen to your Fear. Create an affirmation which you can repeat constantly. My affirmation is ***"I am brave, courageous and fearless because God is always within me, protecting me from the things I fear."*** I repeat this affirmation constantly and it helps me to be relieved of Fear. Whenever you fear anything, create a picture in your mind of God shining his light upon you to give you strength and courage.

39. Seek silence. Silence is the language of God. Your best chance of feeling the Divine Presence is to become silent. Don't be afraid of silence. It helps you to see and feel and to be sensitive to your surroundings. One of the best ways to enter the silent state is through meditation. If thoughts and sounds intrude on your silence, just let them pass out of your mind. If you can become silent, you may receive some suggestions from God that will help you to improve yourself.

40. Know that your life has a purpose. Your are here to show unconditional love to others, to help them as much as

possible and contribute to the improvement of the world. Keep loving and contributing. Follow the motto of "***Service above Self.***"

41. Look forward to getting older. Concentrate on keeping active, healthy, wise and alert. Try to improve your health every year. Visualize the things you will do to bring you joy and happiness, as you grow older. Enjoy your life and keep looking forward to living to 105 years old and passing away in your sleep when you will leave this world with God and go into another world where you will have peace of mind and be completely happy.

    Age is a great thing. Young people don't have enough experience to know how to get the most out of life. Experience is a good teacher and it will make you wiser and help you to become spiritually fit so you will be better able to solve the problems of living and enjoy life more. Remember the older you get the wiser you get.

42. As you get older, be independent. Be your own boss, if possible. Don't let your lover, your friend, or your boss control you. Be free to do your own thing.

43. Enjoy life. Have fun. Appreciate the pleasures of art, music and literature. Keep fresh flowers and beautiful photographs in your home. Enjoy your food and very moderate drinking of alcoholic beverages, coffee, and tea. Be playful. Look for the fun in all situations. Sing, dance and laugh as much as possible.

44. Just as important as physical exercise is mental exercise. Keep working with your mind. Read widely and take an

interest in all things. Keep taking courses on a wide variety of subjects. Engage in stimulating conversation when possible. If you don't have any mentally challenging work or hobbies, do crossword puzzles, play scrabble, study mathematics or write an article on some subject that is of interest to you.

Remember your mind thrives on challenge and dies with inactivity. You can keep your mind active by examining the best seller lists of new books in magazines and newspapers. Pick the stories and concepts which interest you, and read these books. Both fiction and non-fiction can help you to escape temporarily from your problems. Keep trying to increase your knowledge because this will increase your wisdom and will improve your approach to everything in your life. Keep learning. If you stop learning you will age quickly. If you keep learning you will stay young.

45. You don't need the approval of others. You know you are a worthwhile person because you are a spirit from the universe. God is within you, which makes you perfect in one way. Be yourself and don't worry about what others think of you. Be tactful and courteous but do it your way.

46. Writing is therapeutic. If you have a problem, write it down. Any time you feel depressed or unhappy, try to relieve the pressure on yourself by writing about it. This action will help you get it off your mind.

47. If you have something that is worrying you, think of those who have terrible problems, much worse than yours. Think of the people who suffered through the Holocaust and you will realize that your problems will

seem small compared to those who endured this horrible experience. Read the newspapers, listen to the radio, watch television and you will learn of the terrible suffering of the many people around the world. This will help you to put your problems in the right perspective Pray and ask God for help and you will get it.

Remember that adversity is a good thing because when it passes, you will feel better. It takes some adversity to make you appreciate ideal situations. If life was perfect you wouldn't appreciate it as much as you do when you overcome adversities.

Have a symbol which you can activate when you need help. Some visualize that they are a lion or a tiger. My symbol is Humphrey Bogart. When I face adversity, I imagine that I am Humphrey and deal with the situation as I imagine he would.

48. Any assistance and encouragement you can give to those in trouble will start a chain reaction of good feelings. Give to beggars. Help the elderly. Assist those who are struggling to carry heavy parcels or to change a tire. Even to smile at someone who looks worried, or a word of praise will encourage that person and maybe in turn he or she will be sympathetic to others in trouble. If you can find an appropriate opportunity, praise the other person. This will help to build the morale of those who receive it. You could start a chain reaction of happiness in others and this will make you feel good.

49. Happiness is something that every one wants. Unfortunately you can't get it by pursuing it. Buying gifts, drink-

ing, gaining power, having fun and developing skills will only bring you temporary happiness.

The only way to be happy is to set up the attitudes and behavior that will attract it. Here's a formula that should work for you.

1. Bring God into your mind with the power of the Universe flowing through you, which will give you strength and optimism.

2. Surrender to God the things that are making you unhappy.

3. Make a list of all the things in your life for which you are grateful. Keep reviewing this list constantly and keep adding to it

4. Make a list of all the pleasant things that have ever happened to you. Keep reviewing this list and adding to it.

5. Make a list of all the movies and plays you have enjoyed, all the great books you have read and all the great music to which you have listened. Keep constantly reviewing this list and adding to it.

6. List all the wonderful friends you have made and all the interesting people you have met.

7. List all of your exciting family members, brothers and sisters, wives and husbands, children and grandchildren. Keep thinking of all the good times you have had with the family.

8. Discover what activities interest you most and apply yourself passionately to these things either in your work or hobbies. Get your mind off your trivial worries and onto important, pleasant and interesting things.

9. Pray and meditate and ask God to help you to be happy.

10. Concentrate on making other people happy and you will have the best change of becoming happy.

50. In his book *Manifest Your Destiny*, Harper Perennial, Dr. Wayne Dyer describes a program designed to give you anything you want in your life. To achieve this goal, Dr. Dyer recommends that you meditate twice a day for 20 minutes. First thing in the morning, meditate with the mantra "Aaah, Aaah," creating this sound by releasing your breath. This is the sound of Creation. While doing it, concentrate on anything you want to manifest and you may achieve it. In the evening meditation, use the mantra "Ommmm, Ommmm," and concentrate on being thankful for what your meditation is bringing you.

While doing each of these meditations, bring the air up from your "Base Chakra" and imagine you are blowing it out through your "Third Eye," which is in the middle of your forehead. Press your thumbs and forefingers together and for the first seven minutes of your meditation make a noise as you breathe out. During the next seven minutes of your meditation, make a softer noise and during the last seven minutes breathe out as quietly as possible. Success with this meditation is dependent on you living by the principles of spiritual fitness.

This is an oversimplification of this program. To become more informed, get Dr. Dyer's book, *Manifest Your Destiny*, in which he gives complete details on how his method works.

By acting on these fifty thoughts and actions you will be able to help your body to keep healthy. Your body has within it a chemical factory, which is capable of keeping you in excellent mental and physical health, if you can get your subconscious mind to mix the right potion and deliver it to the right place in your body. Visualize yourself being healthy and active. This will stimulate your subconscious mind to give you the right medicine.

To cure yourself of any disability, visualize your body being restored to excellent health with the positive force of God and the Universe traveling through your nerves to cure any disability. Have faith and eliminate fear. With the help of God your mind can do things that seem impossible. Reassure yourself with positive affirmations that you can use to help your body resist disease. Here's an example, ***"I am always in excellent physical, mental and spiritual condition."*** Eliminate all thoughts of disease from your mind and visualize your body as being perfectly healthy.

You might try to bring some magic into keeping yourself healthy. Dr. Wayne Dyer, in his book *Real Magic*, has alerted us to the fact that any of the attitudes or techniques, which have enabled people to perform miracles in the past, are still available. It 's a matter of believing and trusting that you can perform the magic which you are attempting. Jesus said, ***"Even the least among you can do all that I have done and even greater things."***

Why not try for the miracle of keeping yourself in excellent health, as you grow older. Visualize yourself being in excellent physical and mental condition and have the intention to be this way until you eventually pass away in your sleep. See yourself doing this with the power of "light and love" from the Supreme Being helping you. Pray for help, meditate and listen and God will guide you to achieve this magic. Affirm that you can do it and have the intention to do it and get your subconscious mind into the act by constantly repeating this affirmation ***"God will help me to maintain excellent physical and metal health until I am 105, when I will die in my sleep."***

Remember that your body and mind thrive on challenge and slowly die with rest and ease. If you were to stay in bed all the time you would slowly die. There is no way you can rest up and keep healthy. There is no easy way to keep healthy. Your body and mind must be constantly challenged with physical activity and thinking, if you are to keep in good condition. ***"Challenge yourself and live,"*** is a good slogan to help you to improve your health as you grow older.

Have a medical exam at the beginning of each year when you will find out if your health was as good as the year before. If not you will have to search through the fifty ways I have suggested for health improvement. You should also read more on health subjects. Consult with your doctor and psychiatrist and keep searching for ways to get healthier.

More research findings and new knowledge which will be revealed in the future, will help you. This research will be in the areas of food selection, exercising, medication, attitudes, motivation, life style, emotional development and hormones. The new developments for health improvement may be so great that you will be able to improve your health as you grow older. This boggles the mind but some health professionals are predicting it.

Our life expectancy has increased from 47 to nearly 80 years in the last 70 years. If we have learned how to improve our health this much in the past, we should be able to do better in the future with all the new knowledge and technology available.

It's a game. Instead of trying to score a goal, a basket, a touchdown, a home run or a hole in one, you are trying to keep yourself in good physical, mental and spiritual health each year, until you die in your sleep at 105. What a goal! And if you don't win, you still win because you are improving yourself. You have nothing to lose and much to gain. It gives you a goal for your later years. It's a positive approach to your health rather than the negative approach of just letting your body, mind and spirit deteriorate, as you grow older.

In World War II, Victor Frankl, a psychiatrist, was imprisoned in a Nazi Concentration Camp. He was able to survive the horrors of this camp because he had a purpose for surviving. His purpose was to get out of the camp eventually and see his family and tell his story to the world. While in the camp he noticed that those who survived were not the youngest or the healthiest, but those who could find a sense of meaning in this horrible situation, which gave them a purpose to live.

We all need a purpose in life to keep us motivated and interested. Your purpose can be to keep in good physical, mental and spiritual condition each year so you can help others in all your actions at work or play. Always try to contribute something to the world.

This positive approach will give you the feeling of having some control over your health and eventual departure from this world. It will help banish the fear that you have of getting sick in your old age and suffering before you die. It gives you a purpose in life and a goal.

My suggestion to get the fifty health methods working for you is to read them constantly. If you could read them every day, that would be ideal. If not, read them over once a week or once a month. If you do this, the fifty methods of health will become fixed in your mind and become a part of your philosophy of life. You will likely concentrate on several of these fifty methods in your struggle for excellent health. Each person will choose a different set of ideas from the fifty I have presented. That's good.

To get the most out of these methods, I recommend that you also read the following books.

Stopping the Clock, by Ronald Klats, M.D. and Robert Golman, M.D. Keats publishing *Peace, Love & Healing*, by Bernie S. Siegel, M.D., Perennial Library, *Finding the Fountain of Youth*, by Shad Helmstetter, PH.D., Pocket Books, *Real Magic*, by Wayne Dyer, PH.D., Harper Collins, *Timeless Healing*, by Herbert Benson, M.D. Scribner. *Hormonal Health*, by Michael Colgan, O.D. Apple Publishing.

I read the Bible and find it very stimulating and helpful in keeping me on the spiritual path. I also read modern books such as, *Manifest Your Destiny*, by Dr. Wayne Dyer. If we could all follow its concepts and the spiritual principles it prescribes, it would be one of our best paths to spiritual fitness. Other books I read are *Ageless Body, timeless Mind*, by Deepak Choppra, M.D. *Love and Survival* by Dean Ornish M.D., *The Road Less Traveled and Beyond* by M. Scott Peck, M.D. These books are up to date and deal with the spiritual problems of modern life. If you can follow their suggestions, you will come to God.

Best of luck. Search your heart, open your mind, strengthen your faith in God and apply yourself to the most important facets of your life, physical, mental and spiritual health.

THE SEVEN STEPS TO SPIRITUAL FITNESS

What does spirituality mean to me? It's a way of living and believing which has no specific ties to any established religion. This doesn't mean that I believe that religions are wrong. It means that each person based on his specific knowledge, experience, intuition and definite feelings must decide what religion he wants. In what do you have faith? What fits your psychological needs? What do you really believe deep down?

When you become spiritually fit you know that God is with you all the time. You accept the way God is operating the world and you do God's will of loving and helping people and trying to contribute something to the world. As a spiritually fit person, you know that God wants you to surrender to him any problems that you cannot solve yourself. He wants you to leave these problems with him once you have gone all out to solve them and have failed.

When spiritually fit, you will have faith in God to solve your problems that will relieve you of worry. The spiritually fit person worries little because he knows that God is looking after him. He takes reasonable concern for things in his life but he doesn't worry excessively. He delegates his problems to God. Peace of mind is the goal of the spiritually fit person.

The spiritually fit person participates in the world and is concerned with loving others and helping people. If he makes money, gains power, or develops great skills, he doesn't use these things to benefit himself but to help others. In any relationship he doesn't try to win over others but to create a win-win situation by loving and trying to help the other person. The spiritually fit person has his ego under control and he is following the wishes of his Higher Self in his day to day behavior.

The Bible is one of the greatest books that has ever been written. However, men wrote it. God didn't write it. Approximately forty Saints wrote the sixty-six books of the Bible. It is filled with parables and stories. We can all learn much from the Bible, but in my spirituality it isn't the only tool. I take many examples from the Bible but I also try to get God's guidance through meditation and prayer.

In my experience in the business world, I was selling psychological methods of hiring and motivating people, to corporate managers. Rather than going to the Sales, Production, Accounting, or Human Relations departments to sell an idea, I always went to the president of the company first and tried to sell him. Once he was convinced, he would tell the particular department involved that he believed in what I was doing and he would like my proposition examined carefully. This usually resulted in a fair test of my system and ultimately its adoption in many situations.

I am applying the same principle to spirituality. I want to go directly to God. I want to deal with God, not with a mediator.

Churches, temples, synagogues and other religious places, can all be stepping-stones to spiritual fitness and are a great asset to the community. They do many worthwhile spiritual acts and are the strongest supports of spirituality we have. So if you belong to any religious organization, stay with it. You are on the path to spiritual fitness.

Belief in God is the key to spiritual fitness. Each different religion is a route to God. So choose your route or make your own route. That's what I am doing. I am not taking any of the standard well defined and established paths to The Supreme Being. I am bypassing all religions and going directly to God. My style of spirituality is called Godliness.

I believe that God is a God of love. I don't think he is a judging God or a punishing God. In my opinion there are no such places as heaven and hell. God isn't going to punish you for your sins. Instead, he will try to help you understand your sinful ways and change them. If you do anything that you feel is wrong you will punish yourself by mental distress.

God is teaching us to love others, to be tolerant, understanding and forgiving. This is his style, so why would he punish us? God is not a threatening or fearful person. Rather he is understanding and loving and we should love him with unconditional love. I believe God is a higher level type of being, than a human being. He has similar qualities which we humans have but God is much more mature in temperament. He is wiser, more intelligent, more tolerant, more understanding and more loving than a human being.

What does God expect of you? He expects you to love yourself and other men and women and try to contribute something to the world. God's desire for you is joy, happiness and prosperity. He wants you to help the human species evolve into a better type of person by forgiving, loving, caring and serving. My belief is that you should love God and enjoy your life. Just don't do anything that will harm anyone.

Love your fellow men and women and forgive them all for what they have done and serve them by helping them as much as possible. Also contribute to your family, your work situation, your community and your country as much as possible. If you follow this philosophy of life, you will be doing all the things that most religions require and you will please God.

Books give us many theories on religion and spirituality and how great it is to become a spiritual person. Ministers preach sermons and Sunday School teachers make presentations on why we should believe in God. However few people have told us specifically what to do right now to gain the great benefits of spirituality in our lives. That is what I hope I have done. Right here on these pages I have told you of one way to become a spiritual person. Now, in this chapter, I will give you some more information on how to get on the path to spiritual fitness and stay there.

Don't expect a quick immersion into spirituality. Like everything worth while, patience, persistence, experience and faith are required to achieve the joys of the spiritual life. The ultimate goal is spiritual fitness, which is to always feel joyful and happy with peace of mind. This state of mind is difficult to obtain, but the attempt to achieve it will bring you great happiness. So keep on the path. Don't become aggressive or forceful just relax and let it happen. Don't try to make it happen. It may occur in a different way than you expect. This is God guiding you.

Don't expect a smooth fast approach to your ultimate spiritual goal. You will have ups and downs and at times you will wonder if you are on the right track. You may feel that you are not making progress, but you probably are. Keep moving forward, a little bit at a time and you will ultimately get closer to God and spiritual fitness.

From time to time you will get evidence that you are making progress. You may meet someone who is knowledgeable and this person will help you along the path. Or you may surrender in some situation and let God do it, which will relieve you of certain worries. For example, you may have been worried about dying, but by surrendering to God and letting him handle the details you were able to stop worrying.

Don't feel that your contribution to the changing of the human species will not have any power. By behaving in a spiritual manner, you will influence many people in your environment, to change. They in turn will convince others to become spiritual and so you will start a great spiral of changing, which will have an influence on human behavior generally. So realize that your impact on the spiritual world is important.

You will be contributing to making the world a better place in which to live and to developing mankind into a higher type of individual.

Keep remembering that you are not your body or mind or personality. These are states that you dwell in temporarily. The real you is a spirit, which leaves your body when you die. This is why sometimes you can imagine your spirit flying up above your body and observing the worldly you in your day to day performance. The real you is an indestructible spirit that is running your life.

Be aware that your stay in this world is only temporary and it is very difficult to get permanent satisfaction or happiness. Of course, you can have temporary peace of mind and happiness, but constant change, accidents, sickness, the passing away of your best friends and the changing of your environment will always cause you some distress. Your only hope for permanent joy and happiness is the spiritual. If you believe in God and know he is constantly with you, this will bring you the maximum happiness in this world and carry you through death into the next world.

As you move forward in your quest for spiritual fitness your ego will try to trip you up because once you become a spiritual person you will have no more need for the weak behavior of the ego. You will no longer need to triumph over others, make more money, have more material things, be smarter, more skilled and more powerful than others, and to always be right. You will no longer judge others, criticize them or be unforgiving in your attitude.

Incidentally, there is nothing wrong with making money. God wants you to be financially strong, but he wants you to use your money to help others and contribute to the improvement of the world. What God doesn't want you to do is love money, worship it and make it more important than your relationship with Him. He wants you to use your money to advance the causes of spirituality in the world and to help yourself to achieve spiritual fitness. There is nothing wrong with developing skills or achieving a powerful position or winning in any situation, provided you use your skill or power or winning situation to help others rather then to gain advantages for yourself and to defeat others.

Here are more books I have found helpful to keep me on the spiritual path *Love Without Conditions,* by Paul Ferrini, *Words That Heal,* by Douglas Block, *Here and Now*, by Henri Nouwen, *Would you Believe,* by Tom Harpur, *Care For The Soul*, by Thomas Moore, *The Seven Spiritual Laws of Success*, by Deepak Choppra, *Conversations With God,* by Neale Walsch. *Soaring Above the Problems of Life,* by Jack Hartman, *Guilt is the Teacher, Love is the Lesson,* by Joan Borysenko.

Here is a quiz that will give you some idea of how close your are to being spiritually fit.

Do you believe the following?

1. God is always within you and you can trust in God.
2. God loves you and cares for you.
3. God is always guiding you to do what is best for you.
4. God is empowering you and the power of the Universe is flowing through you.
5. If you surrender and let God do it he will help you with your problems.
6. God is operating the world.
7. You have some responsibility for the world and should do everything to keep it clean and well cared for.
8. Witnessing yourself in action in the world will help you to rise above day to day problems.
9. You are a spirit in a body.
10. You should concentrate on ethics, integrity and the process rather than outcome.
11. You adjust to the way God is running the world but often can't understand it.

12. You should ask nothing of the world except "How can I Serve?"
13. Everybody in the world is equal regardless of race, creed, sex, age, physical size, mental capacity, leadership ability, and talent of any kind.
14. The goal of each person should be to love God and love himself and love everyone and contribute to the welfare of others and the community of which he is a part.
15. We are all connected by a spiritual line, which runs from God through everyone.
16. Your intuition is God guiding you.
17. You are wrapped in the "light" of God as you go through life.

Are you taking these actions?

1. Laughing often and trying to see the humor in all situations.
2. Relaxing as you go through life and getting into the pace of the Universe as you do your daily work.
3. Behaving in the world as a trusting, loving person expecting the best from others.
4. Praying constantly. Thanking God for what he has given you and asking for what you need to do his work.
5. Meditating whenever you get the opportunity, to help you connect with God.
6. Always acting positively. Trusting in God that everything will turn out for the best.
7. Following your intuition when it is strongly urging you to take certain action.
8. Exercising and eating mostly fresh fruits, vegetables,

whole grain breads and cereals and some fish and foul.

9. Taking vitamins, herbs and hormones under the supervision of your doctor.
10. Seeking medical advice to try to keep yourself in good health so you can be of service to others.
11. Seeking counseling and taking courses to learn about spirituality and how you can become spiritually fit.
12. Reading books on spirituality and religion.
13. Using affirmations to help you think spiritually.
14. Helping others whenever you get the opportunity and contributing to every situation in which you are involved.

If you answer "yes" to all these statements, you are certainly spirituality fit. It is unlikely you will do this. Only the most spiritually fit person will say "yes" to every statement. However, this questionnaire will alert you to where you can change your thinking or take some action to become spirituality fit. Try and live so you can answer "yes" to all these questions. If you don't believe in some of these statements or actions, pretend that you do. By thinking and acting like a spiritual person, you will become more spiritual and eventually you may come to believe, then to know and have faith and be spiritually fit.

To keep you progressing on the track to spiritual fitness you will need constant chanting, meditation and prayer. Whenever you are in doubt or discouraged with your progress pray and thank God for all he has given you and for guiding and empowering you.

Meditation will help you to contact God and keep you conscious that he is always within you. Chanting will give you another way to keep in touch with God. Keep praying and ask God to help you to become a more spiritual being.

If you do attain spiritual fitness, don't expect all the problems of living to be solved. You will still have work to do. You will still have some people problems and you will still have some worry and distress. Spiritual fitness will not change the world for you but it will give you new attitudes towards it, which will help you to move through life with less friction and worry. You will find the problems of life easier to solve when you become spiritually fit and apply the attitudes of the Higher Self to your day to day living.

Your ego will be using every bit of its creative power to thwart you in your struggle towards spiritual fitness. The only way you can defend yourself against this onslaught is to have some spiritual ideas that are more desirable than the ego's ideas. You don't want to destroy the ego, but to get control of it. The ego isn't who you really are, it is who you are trying to be. If you control your mind, you can push out all the negative thoughts which your ego throws at you.

Your ego believes that you are separate from others and that you are not connected with God or with other people. Your ego is always trying to prove that you are better than others. The ego wants you to win, achieve, develop your skills and make money. Your Higher Self is not concerned with worldly gains but with how you can be of service to others. It knows that you are connected with God and with every person in the world and that we are all equal.

Finally, you have seven important steps with affirmations to keep your ego under control and keep you on the path to spiritual fitness. Memorize these seven steps and keep thinking of them, constantly. These are important guides to spiritual fitness. When you believe these seven statements and live by them constantly, you are spiritually fit.

Here they are.

1. "God is always within me, loving me and caring for me."
2. "The power of the Universe is flowing through me, giving me the strength and energy to survive any adversity and remain positive and optimistic"
3. "God is constantly guiding me"
4. "God is helping me to surrender to him the problems I cannot solve myself. He will solve these problems for me."
5. "God is empowering me to adjust to his way of operating the world."
6. "The "light" of God is shining down upon me, collaborating with my subconscious mind and its parts to protect me from the hostilities, criticisms and discouragement of the world and to give me the wisdom, strength and energy to do God's will."
7. "I visualize and intend to live the rest of my life with God guiding me. I see myself in action, with the "light" of God shining down upon me and bringing me unlimited and unconditional love, which I can share with others as I go through life with excellent physical, mental and spiritual health until I die in my sleep at age 105 or sometime near that age."

With the suggested thoughts and actions I have given you, worry about sickness and death should not bother you, as you grow older. You will have faith in God's willingness to guide you and look after you. Surrender to him and stop worrying about the future. He wants to help you but you have to believe and trust and ask him for help in your prayers.

Dwell on these seven steps constantly and visualize it all happening. If you don't believe it, pretend that you do. What you need most, as you grow older is a goal to believe in and a purpose in life. I have suggested to you the goal of keeping in excellent physical, mental and spiritual health, so you can help others and contribute something to the world.

Whenever you get any negative thoughts, switch to this positive scenario. Visualize it all happening in large colorful dynamic pictures and intend that it will happen and it will.

As I have written before, I don't expect you to follow my program exactly. I give it to you to suggest some ideas on how to develop your own program.

Your spiritual life is a very personal thing. Everyone has different attitudes, motivation, intelligence and emotional maturity, so there is no formula for spirituality that fits everyone's needs. There are about six billion people in the world so maybe there should be six billion different religions so each person can have a belief that is right for him. This is ridiculous, of course, but it makes you think of how somebody else cannot tell you what spiritual way is right for you.

Remember that I am not a prophet, saint, guru, minister, priest, rabbi, doctor, psychiatrist or clinical psychologist, nor do I have any formal education in the spiritual field, nor am I completely spiritually fit myself. I am only on the path to spiritual fitness. So check with your spiritual counselor, before you make any changes in your beliefs or your attitudes and with your medical doctor, before you make any changes in your physical activities diet or your life style.

Don't forget there are many paths to spiritual fitness through Christ, Mother Teresa, Muhammad, Confucius and others. There are also hundreds of religious organizations which can lead you to God. Keep on whatever route suits you. I am not trying to convert you or change your beliefs. My path to spiritual fitness is only one of many. What is important is that you get to God. My form of spirituality I call Godliness.

Keep constantly using my short prayer or some version of it. ***"Thank you God. I love you, God. Forgive me, God. Help me, God. Help others God, I am grateful to you, God."***

Good luck. I love you. God bless you and guide you along the path to spiritual fitness.

The final end and purpose of every human being is the unitive knowledge of God's being.

Aldous Huxley 1894-1963

The supreme value and highest good is not life as such, but spiritual life rising up to God.

Nicholas Berdyaen 1874-1981

The meaning of life consists in the love and service of God.

Leo Tolstoy 1828-1910

Heaven means to be one with God.

Confucius

JACK H. McQUAIG

Jack McQuaig has spent his life helping people to find their goals and achieve them. As an Industrial Psychologist, he has advised management in organizations of all sizes how to bring better methods of hiring and training into their businesses.

Author of eight books on management and physical and mental fitness, his concern has always been to help people to be more effective at their work. A masters degree in psychology and a lifetime of appraising and motivating personnel have given him insight into what makes people happy and successful.

Since his semi-retirement, he has turned to the study of spirituality to find more help in gaining happiness and peace of mind. His conclusion is that achieving material things, gaining power and developing skills do not give the answers to the most important things in life.

Jack McQuaig's purpose in writing this book is to try and simplify spirituality so more people can benefit from it. He has developed a simple formula which men and women of all beliefs and those who have no spiritual beliefs can use to move forward on the path to spiritual fitness.

Without any formal training in religious thinking, he brings to this book a new and fresh approach to spirituality, free from the traditional format of established religions.

He accepts all religions and is not trying to change anyone's beliefs but to help everyone along the path to God. He believes that all religions are needed because there are so many variations in the way people react to God. He believes that spirituality is a very personal thing, and that each person must search to find what he believes and follow his own thinking.

People who read this book should get a new insight into spirituality, which will help them to achieve spiritual fitness.

AGMV MARQUIS
Québec, Canada
2000